| | DATE DUE | | |
|---|---|---|---|
| | | | |
| | | | |
| | | | |
| | | | |
| | | | |
| | | | |
| | | | |
| | | | |
| | | | |
| | | | |
| | | | |

# SCOTT HAMILTON

OVERCOMING ADVERSITY

# SCOTT HAMILTON

Kristine Brennan

Chelsea House Publishers

Philadelphia

*Frontis: Scott Hamilton, one of the greatest and most beloved figure skaters of all time, overcame serious illnesses both in childhood and as an adult.*

## CHELSEA HOUSE PUBLISHERS

EDITOR IN CHIEF  Stephen Reginald
MANAGING EDITOR  James D. Gallagher
PRODUCTION MANAGER  Pamela Loos
ART DIRECTOR  Sara Davis
DIRECTOR OF PHOTOGRAPHY  Judy L. Hasday
SENIOR PRODUCTION EDITOR  Lisa Chippendale

*Staff for* **Scott Hamilton**
SENIOR EDITOR  James D. Gallagher
ASSOCIATE ART DIRECTOR  Takeshi Takahashi
DESIGNER  Brian Wible
PICTURE RESEARCHER  Sandy Jones
COVER DESIGN  Keith Trego

First Printing

1 3 5 7 9 8 6 4 2

Library of Congress Cataloging-in-Publication Data

Brennan, Kristine.
Scott Hamilton / by Kristine Brennan.
112 pp. cm. — (Overcoming adversity)
Includes bibliographical references (p. 105) and index.
Summary: A biography of the accomplished figure skater Scott Hamilton,
covering his life, career, and battle with testicular cancer.
ISBN 0-7910-4944-2 — ISBN 0-7910-4945-0
1. Hamilton, Scott, 1958-   —Juvenile literature. 2. Skaters—United States—
Biography—Juvenile literature. [1. Hamilton, Scott, 1958-
2. Ice Skaters.] I. Title. II. Series.
GV850.H33B74 1998
796.91'2'092—dc21
[b]                                                           98-37285
                                                              CIP
                                                              AC

# CONTENTS

# OVERCOMING ADVERSITY

# ON FACING ADVERSITY

*James Scott Brady*

I GUESS IT'S a long way from a Centralia, Illinois, train yard to the George Washington University Hospital Trauma Unit. My dad was a yardmaster for the old Chicago, Burlington & Quincy Railroad. As a child, I used to get to sit in the engineer's lap and imagine what it was like to drive that train. I guess I always have liked being in the "driver's seat."

Years later, however, my interest turned from driving trains to driving campaigns. In 1979, former Texas governor John Connally hired me as a press secretary in his campaign for the American presidency. We lost the Republican primary to a former Hollywood star named Ronald Reagan. But I managed to jump over to the Reagan campaign. When Reagan was elected in 1980, I was "sitting in the catbird seat," as humorist James Thurber would say—poised to be named presidential press secretary. I held that title throughout the eight years of the Reagan administration. But not without one terrible, extended interruption.

It happened barely two months after the Reagan administration took office. I never even heard the shots. On March 30, 1981, my life went blank in an instant. In an attempt to assassinate President Reagan, John Hinckley Jr. armed himself with a "Saturday night special"—a low-quality, $29 pistol—and shot wildly as our presidential entourage exited a Washington hotel. One of the exploding bullets struck me just above the left eye. It shattered into a couple dozen fragments, some of which penetrated my skull and entered my brain.

The next few months of my life were a nightmare of repeated surgery, broken contact with the outside world, and a variety of medical complications. More than once, I was very close to death.

The next few years were filled with frustrating struggles to function with a paralyzed right side, struggles to speak and communicate.

To people who face and defeat daunting obstacles, "ambition" is not becoming wealthy or famous or winning elections or awards. Words like "ambition" and "achievement" and "success" take on very different meanings. The objective is just to live, to wake up every morning. The goals are not lofty; they are very ordinary.

My own heroes are ordinary folks—but they accomplish extraordinary things because they try. My greatest hero is my wife, Sarah. She's accomplished a lot of things in life, but two stand out. The first has been the way she has cared for me and our son since I was shot. A tremendous tragedy and burden was dropped unexpectedly into her life, totally beyond her control and without justification. She could have given up; instead, she focused her energies on preserving our family and returning our lives to normal as much as possible. Week by week, month by month, year by year, she has not reached for the miraculous, just for the normal. Yet in focusing on the normal, she has helped accomplish the miraculous.

Her other most remarkable accomplishment, to me, has been spearheading the effort to keep guns out of the hands of criminals and children in America. Opponents call her a "gun grabber"; I call her a national hero. And I am not alone.

After a seven-year battle, during which Sarah and I worked tirelessly to educate the public about the need for stronger gun laws, the Brady Bill became law in 1993. It was a victory, achieved in the face of tremendous opposition, that now benefits all Americans. From the time the law took effect through fall 1997, background checks had stopped 173,000 criminals and other high-risk purchasers from buying handguns, and the law has helped to reduce illegal gun trafficking.

Sarah was not pursuing fame, or even recognition. She simply started at one point—when our son, Scott, found a loaded handgun on the seat of a pickup truck and, thinking it was a toy, pointed it at Sarah.

Fortunately, no one was hurt. But seeing a gun nearly bring a second tragedy upon our family, Sarah became determined to do whatever she could to prevent senseless death and injury from guns.

Some people think of Sarah as a powerful political force. To me, she's the person who so many times fed me and helped me dress during my long years of recovery.

Overcoming obstacles is part of life, not just for people who are challenged by disabilities, illnesses, or tragedies, but for all people. No matter what the obstacle—fear, disability, prejudice, grief, or a difficulty that isn't likely to "just go away"—we can all work to make this world a better place.

*Triumphant return: As cheers from 10,000 fans roll across the ice, Scott Hamilton exults in completing his first skating performance after being diagnosed with cancer seven months earlier.*

# 1

## "I WIN"

*I firmly believe that the only disability in life is a bad attitude.*
—Scott Hamilton, 1997

ON WEDNESDAY, OCTOBER 29, 1997, Scott Hamilton skated before approximately 10,000 enthralled onlookers at the Great Western Forum in Inglewood, California. As usual, the audience was pulling for the 1984 Olympic gold medalist from the moment he took the ice.

This was hardly a routine performance. Although Hamilton was one of the most seasoned figure skaters in the sport, he had admitted in a phone interview the day before that he was suffering from something more than preperformance jitters. "I'm scared to death," he said. "It's going to be different from any other show." As he skated onto the ice Hamilton wore a simple, let's-get-down-to-business outfit: black pants and a white shirt. Tears shone in his eyes, and the audience sprang to their feet before he even hit his starting pose. As the song "With One More Look at You" began to fill the Forum, Scott Hamilton opened his first performance since a seven-month battle with testicular cancer had interrupted his career and threatened his life.

After doctors found a large tumor in his abdomen in March 1997, the popular skater endured four rounds of chemotherapy intended to reduce the size of the cancer. By June, the tumor had shrunk to an operable size, allowing surgeons to make an incision from Hamilton's breastbone to his groin area to remove both the tumor and his right testicle. "The drugs knock you out, make you sick. It really robs you of your strength and conviction," he told *USA Today* during his recovery. He was medically released to skate again on August 1, but didn't feel strong enough to do so for several days.

Hamilton's first day on the ice had been a rude awakening: he was weak, down to a slight 115 pounds on his 5-foot 3-1/2-inch frame, and bald after shaving his head when his hair started to fall out during chemotherapy. "I couldn't do a thing," he recalled. Even after months of training, as he put the finishing touches on his comeback exhibition, his body did not cooperate as it had before cancer. "I haven't gotten everything back yet," he told an interviewer. "My stamina is really weak from all the chemotherapy and radiation. My blood counts still aren't normal. It's going to take a lot of work."

Scott Hamilton has never been a stranger to hard work. The feat of skating before an audience just seven months after his diagnosis was a testament to his iron will. Even if it would take some time for Hamilton to climb back to his former level of technical prowess, his outstanding character guaranteed him a permanent place in the hearts of his fans.

As he struggled to regain all of his lost skills, Scott Hamilton enjoyed worldwide support, receiving over 55,000 get-well cards. "It was remarkable. It was dramatic," he said of the widespread response to his illness and recovery. He also had the warm thoughts of his distinguished Stars on Ice costars: Ekaterina Gordeeva, Katarina Witt, Kristi Yamaguchi, Brian Boitano, Kurt Browning,

Brian Orser, Paul Wylie, and Rosalynn Sumners. Before Hamilton took the ice at the Forum, they had performed to celebrate the return of their honorary leader.

The crowd, too, boasted its share of luminaries. Movie legend Jack Nicholson and supermodel Cindy Crawford were among the fans who had come out to see their champion conquer his toughest opponent to date.

The star attraction began to skate—and to end all talk of the toll that cancer had taken on him. As he began to glide across the ice, the spectators knew that Scott Hamilton's magic was back after less than three months of reconditioning.

His musical selection, "With One More Look at You," which was originally performed by Barbra Streisand in the movie *A Star is Born*, was a subdued choice for Hamilton. He had asked country artist Gary Morris to sing a new version of the ballad for two very personal reasons. The

*Hamilton thanked the Cleveland Clinic, where he had been treated for testicular cancer in the spring and summer of 1997, by donating the proceeds of his first post-cancer skating appearance to the institution.*

*Skating a grueling four-and-a-half-minute program to the song "With One More Look at You," Scott Hamilton dazzled the crowd with breathtaking spins and triple jumps. When he was finished, Hamilton, who had been training for less than three months after his cancer treatment ended, still had enough energy to do his signature move: a back-flip.*

song's title reflected his deepest longing: "Just to be there one more time center ice, looking at an audience and being able to entertain them was the reason for putting this show together," he had said. "With One More Look at You" also reminded Scott Hamilton of someone he missed very much. Streisand's original version of the song had been released around the time that his mother, Dorothy, lost her own battle with cancer 20 years earlier. Although the song had greatly affected him then, Scott was not permitted to skate to it in amateur competition because it included vocals.

But on this fall night in 1997, Scott Hamilton, the unofficial king of professional figure skating, was expressing his deepest feelings on the ice—his way. He skated a grueling four-and-a-half-minute routine—the length of the men's long program in competition, enough to tax the strength of a skater in peak condition. When he attempted a triple toe loop, Hamilton fell. His audience burst into applause, and urged him to carry on.

The gesture was hardly necessary: Hamilton went on to land two other triple jumps as his routine drew to a close. The slight, weakened man who could scarcely do a spin just weeks earlier was now pulling off triples at the end of a full-length routine. Scott Hamilton took a microphone in hand after he finished his program, closed his eyes as the audience's cheers soared through the Forum, and then, in a breaking voice, said simply, "I win."

"It wasn't my best," he continued, skating slowly. "It wasn't about being 100 percent. It was about standing between these lights and having the greatest view in the world." Scott Hamilton wasn't finished amazing his fans yet, though. Gaining speed as he spoke, Hamilton said, "But I wouldn't truly be *back* . . ." and successfully executed a backflip—a potentially dangerous move that has been his trademark for years.

His skate that night was a poignant thank-you to his fans for their love and support. But Hamilton also had individuals to thank—most notably his longtime girlfriend, Karen Plage, whom he pointed out in the crowd. As she stood up, Hamilton credited her with helping him survive and come back from his ordeal.

In the general euphoria that followed his return to the ice, Scott Hamilton did not forget those who were still fighting to regain their health. He had, after all, been one of them only a short time ago. "Tonight was about control, getting back on the ice so everybody sitting in a hospital bed with an IV bag in their arm knows there is an end in sight," he said. His actions backed up his words: proceeds

*Scott Hamilton has never allowed adversity to stop him from becoming the best; at the same time, he does not dwell on the cancer that threatened his life in 1997. "Every day, I'm thankful for my health; every day, I'm grateful there was treatment and a cure for what happened to me," he told USA* Today *in February 1998. "At the same time, that's behind me. It's time to get back to a normal life. On one level, I feel so fortunate to be able to get through it as well as I did. At the same time, I can't allow that to take over."*

from Hamilton's comeback exhibition were donated to the Cleveland Clinic Foundation. He had gone to the Cleveland Clinic to confirm his cancer diagnosis and had taken his chemotherapy treatments there. Now he was making a point of giving back.

This was no surprise to those who knew Scott Hamilton. The countless fans who had followed his world-class skating career over the previous 20 years were not exactly shocked, either. Since his amateur days, he had carved out a unique niche for himself as a skater with an instinctive desire to give crowds what they wanted. "If figure skating purists aren't so hot about back flips on the ice, but the audience goes wild for them, you know what Hamilton will do: back flips at the start and end of every show," read an article in the *Milwaukee Journal Sentinel* about Scott's professional work with Stars on Ice.

Hamilton's generous spirit went beyond crowd-pleasing stunts, however. He was a longtime participant in benefits for the American Cancer Society in his mother's memory. Moreover, Stars on Ice, the professional touring company cofounded by Hamilton, regularly raised money for the Make-A-Wish Foundation, a charity that grants the wishes of seriously and terminally ill children.

Years earlier, Hamilton himself had been a sick child with a dream. A mysterious boyhood ailment forced Scott Hamilton to linger in a world of solitude, quiet indoor play, and hospitals until the age of nine. The illness stunted his growth, but it also spurred his desire to become a great skater after his recovery. The sickly boy who once inspired worry in everyone he met had transformed himself by 1984 into an Olympic gold medalist who evoked awe in everyone who watched him perform. Along the way, Hamilton also racked up four consecutive United States and World Championship figure skating titles.

Other skaters might have chosen to bask in the rewards that followed; not Hamilton. The sacrifices and losses he weathered in his quest for Olympic glory—including the death of his mother, who never got to see Scott climb the medals podium—fortified him against despair when setbacks befell him in later years. He continued to be an outspoken ambassador for his sport on the professional level as both a performer and a commentator. Most important, he continued winning fans with his characteristic grace and humor.

Never was the strength of Scott Hamilton's character more rigorously tested than during his battle with cancer. Judging by the cheering of the crowd that shared his return to the ice in Inglewood, his character had passed this latest test with flying colors.

*Doctors were never able to definitively determine the cause of a childhood illness that halted Scott Hamilton's growth when he was two years old. Scott suffered from this problem until he was nine. Hamilton's short stature can be seen in this picture with rival David Santee, a head taller than Scott, as they skate around the rink together after the 1981 World Championships. In this competition, as he would throughout his career, Hamilton proved that size doesn't matter: he placed first and Santee placed second.*

# 2

# AN UNLIKELY OLYMPIAN

ON AUGUST 28, 1958, a five-pound, seven-ounce baby boy was born in Toledo, Ohio. Although a bit small, he was normal and healthy in every way, according to the Lucas County Child and Family Services Agency.

Some 20 miles away, Dorothy and Ernest Hamilton longed for a child to join their five-year-old daughter, Susan. The two teachers had wanted a large family since their 1951 marriage. But after a series of miscarriages following Susan's birth, culminating in despair for Dorothy and her husband when she gave birth to a baby boy, Donald, who survived only eight hours, the Hamiltons decided to enlarge their family through adoption and contacted the Lucas County agency.

In October of 1958, the lives of the lightweight baby boy and the hopeful couple intersected forever. The newly named Scott Scovell Hamilton came to live with Dorothy, Ernest, and Susan at 257 State Street in Bowling Green, Ohio. Dr. Hamilton was a biology professor at Bowling Green State University and Mrs. Hamilton was a second-grade teacher. They had thoughtfully prepared their little girl for her new brother's homecoming with age-appropriate books and plenty of discussion. The reality of a skinny, shrivelled newborn fell far short of Susan's expectations, however.

Although "Scotty" would never flesh out to become a plump baby, he had charm and vitality from the start. Before long, Susan Hamilton proudly displayed her infant brother during show-and-tell at her school.

As Scott progressed rapidly from crawling to running, Ernie Hamilton faced the challenge of keeping the energetic little boy out of harm's way. Scott's small size belied great strength and agility: not long after Scott took up residence in his crib, Dr. Hamilton had to build a lid for it to prevent him from vaulting over the sides. His parents could not rely on supposedly childproof gates or playpens to contain Scott, either. He was capable of seemingly impossible acrobatics for a boy of his age and size. When Scott was two years old, his father inadvertently left a ladder propped up against the side of the family's three-bedroom house after finishing some repairs: a horrified Ernie never repeated this mistake after spotting his dexterous toddler on the roof. Dorothy Hamilton's searches for Scott frequently ended in a kitchen cabinet over the refrigerator—some six feet off the ground.

Although Scott Hamilton's athleticism and fearlessness were apparent from a young age, there was still little about him that suggested his future profession. His first experience on skates, in fact, seemed destined to be his last as well. "I never wanted to skate again," Hamilton told biographer Michael Steere after recounting a spill on a neighbor's frozen driveway at around four years of age: "I fell off my skates and landed on my head and cried for two hours."

Ice-skating traumas notwithstanding, Scott had no trouble keeping up with the neighborhood kids during his early childhood. Still, his parents were concerned because Scott was not growing. "Everything went beautifully with Scotty until he was two years old," Ernie Hamilton told

*Sports Illustrated* in 1984. "And then, just like that, he stopped growing." Scott's small stature became even more apparent at age four when the Hamiltons adopted another baby, Steven, into their family. Steven was soon bigger than his older brother.

"We were stricken," Ernie Hamilton later recalled of the years of medical detective work that followed. Only one thing was certain: Scott was not adequately absorbing nutrients from the food he ate. Doctors estimated that two-thirds of his intestinal tract was paralyzed, but could not agree upon the cause of the little boy's illness.

The initial diagnosis was celiac disease, a condition that renders the small intestine incapable of properly digesting foods containing gluten, which is found in wheat, rye, oats, and barley. Scott began following a milk- and gluten-free diet when he was in the first grade. Dorothy Hamilton learned to prepare foods using rice and soy flour. Scott, however, found his severely restricted diet unappealing. School presented the added torture of watching his friends eat sandwiches on white bread, cookies, and other brown-bag treats that were forbidden to him. In grade school, Scott Hamilton's only consolation was special permission to drink soda during classes to boost his energy level.

The gluten-free diet didn't help. Scott's father later said that his doctors only managed "to starve the poor little kid." Eventually, a family friend and physician named Andrew Klepner struck a serious blow against the theory that Scott had celiac disease. The Hamiltons and the Klepners were vacationing together when Dr. Klepner convinced Ernie and Dorothy to let Scott eat the same food as everyone else. After Scott got over his initial nervousness and dug in, he suffered no ill effects. Even so, the cause of his retarded physical growth remained a mystery.

During Scott's first-grade year, the Hamiltons moved to a bigger house that they had built on Bowling Green's Brownwood Drive. As he moved through the second and third grades at the Kenwood School, Scott's health deteri-

*Ernie Hamilton, Scott's adopted father, was a biology professor at Bowling Green University. He and his wife, Dorothy, Scott's mother, spent years trying to track down the cause of Scott's medical condition.*

*Children's Hospital in Boston was one of the many medical centers where doctors attempted to find out why young Scott had stopped growing.*

orated rapidly. He was not a distinguished student; he struggled just to stay alert during classroom lessons. Although he longed to run and play ball outside at recess he could no longer keep up with his bigger, stronger peers, who sometimes teased him about his size. The general consensus among those who knew Scott during these discouraging years, however, was that he was friendly and uncomplaining despite the isolation his illness had imposed upon him.

By this time, his young life was also regularly disrupted by hospitalizations. He remembers bedeviling the nurses assigned to his care, and he credits his frequent stays away from his family with making him self-sufficient. But Hamilton's childhood ordeal also fostered an intense hatred of hospitals—a hatred that cancer would one day force him to reexamine. "Scott's memories from those dark years are like those of an enemy of a harsh regime—stretches of lone confinement broken by torture," wrote Michael Steere in his 1985 biography of Hamilton. "Even to this day he detests hospitals; the smell of hospital disinfectant is enough to upset him."

The seemingly endless evaluations Scott endured yielded a new diagnosis: cystic fibrosis (CF). Cystic fibrosis is a genetic defect that causes affected children to secrete excessive mucus. Those with CF also suffer from congestion of the lungs and pancreatic ducts, which prevents them from breathing freely or digesting fats and proteins. Three factors in addition to Scott's obvious emaciation suggested this frightening condition: his birth records indicated a history of CF in his biological father's family, he seemed to have lung problems, and he tested positive for a recessive gene that causes the disease. However, further tests showed that this diagnosis was another medical dead end. Scott did not have cystic fibrosis.

At Dr. Klepner's urging, the Hamiltons took Scott to Children's Hospital in Boston over the Christmas holidays of 1967. Dorothy and Ernest incorporated the trip into a visit with relatives in Massachusetts. At Children's Hospital, Scott was examined by Dr. Harry Schwachman, a well-known specialist in pediatric gastrointestinal illnesses. Dr. Schwachman had identified a malabsorption ailment that bore his own name—Schwachman's syndrome—but he did not think that Scott's symptoms fitted the clinical picture of this illness. (Schwachman's syndrome is indicated by a cluster of symptoms that include dwarfism and pancreatic failure.)

After his visit to Children's Hospital, Scott Hamilton's

medical history becomes murky. Before the 1984
Olympics, Ernie Hamilton told *Sports Illustrated* that
Scott did in fact have Schwachman's syndrome; Scott has
since stated that he did not have the disease. Other
accounts of Hamilton's childhood identify his illness as
Schwachman's. Most retellings of Scott's early life story
agree on two things: a death sentence handed down by
doctors—one doctor said he had one year to live, another
reportedly said that he only had six months—and the fact
that he suffered from intestinal paralysis that interfered
with his nutrition and growth. In his biography *Scott
Hamilton*, Michael Steere writes that Dr. Schwachman
believed Scott's illness was rooted in extreme anxiety and
depression:

> The Hamiltons went home to Bowling Green. In January,
> Dorothy wrote to Dr. Schwachman. She thanked him for
> getting to the root of Scott's problem and letting the fam-
> ily know, after all those years of diets and treatments and
> medication, that Scott did not have a serious medical con-
> dition. Scott was about to begin seeing a child psychiatrist,
> she wrote, and his appetite had doubled.

Despite the many contradicting accounts of Scott's illness and recovery, two things are clear. First, his physical
symptoms were real, whatever their cause; second, Scott's
health reached a state of crisis before it got better. By the
time he was eight years old, a feeding tube snaked into his
stomach via his right nostril. When he wasn't connected to
a bag of liquid nutrient solution that hung from an IV pole,
Scott wore the feeding tube tucked and taped behind his
left ear. When Scott could no longer stand being lashed to
the pole while the solution dripped slowly through his
nasogastric tube, he would adjust the drip so that the fluid
gushed in quickly.

During the Hamilton family's trip to Boston, Dorothy
tried to take her son's mind off of such torturous treatments
by taking him to an ice show. A skater named Freddie Tren-
kler entertained the audience with a comedic routine, no

doubt providing Scott with a welcome respite from the anxiety surrounding his trip to the hospital. Hamilton himself would one day build his own skating reputation by pleasing crowds first and judges second.

In late 1967, nobody would ever have predicted Scott Hamilton's golden future. The invisible hand of fate seemed to be laying the groundwork for his destiny, however. While he was languishing with an illness that nobody could name, Bowling Green State University was building an ice arena with an eye to starting a collegiate hockey program. The rink was completed and opened to the public in 1967.

Scott's first meeting with the ice was not really planned. One Saturday in November, Susan was supposed to go skating with Dr. Klepner's two daughters when nine-year-old Scott decided that he wanted to tag along. Dorothy Hamilton swallowed her fear that something might happen to her frail middle child and allowed him to skate.

The chain of events to follow would surpass her wildest dreams.

*Years of practice began to pay off in 1976 as Scott Hamilton won the U.S. Junior National Championship in Colorado Springs, Colorado, that year.*

# 3

# THE GREAT EQUALIZER

*Because of my size, my center of balance, I would pick things up*
*quicker than kids who were much taller than I was.*
—Scott Hamilton, on how his small stature
became an asset to his skating

AFTER THAT VISIT to the rink, the boy who as a preschooler had never wanted to skate again now couldn't get enough ice time. Dorothy and Ernie Hamilton gladly paid for a club membership and Saturday morning lessons at the Bowling Green Skating Club. "You'd race, play tag, play whip," Hamilton later recalled. "You could play a lot of things, so for me, just to go out every Saturday morning and skate with a bunch of kids my age and to learn new things was pretty exciting."

At last, Scott had found a place where size and strength were unimportant: the quarter-inch steel blades strapped to his feet were a great equalizer between him and the other kids. In an interview with Pat Summerall, Hamilton explained the new lease on life that came with learning to glide across the ice:

[W]hat skating really offered me was a way to challenge myself and to be involved in something that was active and physical, and it gave me a real good sense of self-esteem. Because of my size, my center of balance, I would pick things up quicker than kids who were much taller than I was. So it gave me a great deal. It was something I could do as well as or better than all the other guys that I couldn't compete with in football or basketball. So it was physical and emotional.

At first, the confidence that their son gained by skating was good enough for the Hamiltons; but they also got a miracle in the bargain. "Everybody in figure skating knows the rest of the story," wrote Bob Ottum in a 1984 *Sports Illustrated* profile of Hamilton, "but nobody knows what happened to the ailment." Scott's incredulous doctor declared him healthy during a checkup in 1968. He had even started growing again, although he would never completely catch up with other boys his age.

To his grateful family, Scott's abbreviated height was a trivial matter. They maintained that the combination of the ice arena's cool, moist air and the rigors of skating saved his life. Out came the feeding tube. Gone was the omnipresent cloud of sickness that had hung over Scott Hamilton's head for most of his childhood. This newfound good health paved the way for his natural exuberance to come to the fore. The lethargic third grader who could barely stay alert in class gave way to a spirited fourth grader with a flair for teasing and wisecracking. Scott was not much of a troublemaker at school, though. He remembers himself instead as "the kind of kid who liked to show off and do a lot of things."

Skating was a natural extension of his youthful clowning. Hamilton's first skating teacher was Rita Lowery, an ice-skating professional who taught at the Bowling Green Skating Club with her husband, David. Scott's innate understanding of how to position his body on the ice caught her eye; the young student's boundless enthusiasm

Scott's first skating instruc-
tors, Rita and David Lowery,
soon knew that their young
student had a special talent
for figure skating. Hamilton
seemed to have an instinctive
understanding of how to place
himself on the ice, Rita later
recalled.

for skating did not escape her notice, either. Scott attended extra open skating sessions, as well as the Saturday
group lessons, in order to apply what he'd learned. Lowery knew that Scott's natural sense of what to do on
skates—combined with his willingness to keep trying—
held much more promise over time than an ability to pick
up tricks quickly. The Lowerys alerted the Hamiltons to
Scott's talent. Soon he was taking private lessons with Rita
for a half hour each day.

Fifteen minutes of each lesson was devoted to figures.
In figures, a skater works on one "patch" of ice to trace
patterns on the ice using different edges of his or her skate
blades. The skater's use of the proper edge and the preci-

*With Hamilton's first tentative
steps onto the ice at the
Bowling Green Ice Arena, he
entered a new world where
his short stature no longer
mattered.*

sion of the completed figure determines the score. Such a
controlled, concentrated effort challenged Scott's nine-
year-old attention span. Rita Lowery often had to remind
him to slow down.

Although Scott preferred the 15-minute freeskating part
of each lesson, Mrs. Lowery knew how important compulsory figures would be if Scott wanted to go on with his
skating. The compulsory figures segment of amateur figure skating competitions counted for half of a skater's total
score until 1973, then dropped from 30 percent to 20 percent of the total score during the course of Scott's amateur
career. (Figures are no longer required in competitions.)
Mastery of figures was also required for tests administered
by the United States Figure Skating Association (USFSA)
that determined a skater's competition class. Figure skating has classes based on skill level: Subjuvenile, Juvenile,
Intermediate, Novice, Junior, and Senior.

In the spring of 1968, Scott had not yet taken his first

figures test. He skated in his first exhibition when he took part in Bowling Green's annual Ice Horizons show. Scott was in a routine that required him to fall so that another skater playing the hero would prevail. His turn to shine was yet to come.

People could see a budding showman in Scott even when he played a supporting role. His enthusiasm was contagious long before his skating became polished. He grabbed a little bit of the spotlight for himself while still at the Subjuvenile level when he won second place in a competition that summer. It was an impressive showing for a boy who, just one year earlier, was widely believed to be dying.

As Scott's involvement with skating increased, so did his family's. His big sister Sue did some ice dancing—as did Scott, until the girls he was paired with grew too tall for him—but she broke her arm trying to do a jump that Scott taught her. Dorothy Hamilton was the parent who went to competitions with Scott; Ernie couldn't bring himself to do it. "I'd get so nervous for Scotty, and there was nothing I could do to help him out there," the doting father later told *Sports Illustrated*. Instead, Ernie built props and scenery for the annual Ice Horizons shows, an activity he continued even after Scott's ascent to stardom.

Figure skating is an expensive sport, and the Hamiltons were forced to make changes in their daily lives so that Scott could continue skating. In addition to coaching fees and the cost of ice time, there were skates and costumes to pay for. When Scott competed away from home, there were travel expenses. Dorothy went back to school for an advanced education degree at Bowling Green, which led to a university professorship in home economics that paid better than her elementary school teaching job. The family would also eventually put a second mortgage on their house to keep Scott on the ice.

Scott's skating also drove the Hamiltons to make hard decisions about how to divide their most precious

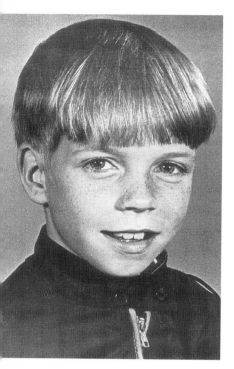

*Under the tutelage of Herb Plata, Scott won the 1970 Eastern Great Lakes Regional competition.*

resource—their time—between all three of their children. The scale often tipped in Scott's favor. Michael Steere writes:

> The facts at this stage suggest an unattractive picture of Scott: a spoiled mama's boy, Little Lord Figure Skater. . . . The unattractive picture does not fit him at all. Those who remember his boyhood are unanimous in saying that Scott, at any age, was not spoiled. . . . He was polite, pleasant, cheery, kind—as if by virtue of an indestructible good character.

No doubt he brought those personal qualities to the 1969 Ice Horizons show. The press had already gotten wind of Bowling Green's "miracle child." Scott's return from what seemed to be the brink of death was a story that would be told and retold throughout his skating career. Ten-year-old Scott was a charmer in his first featured performance, his blond bangs peeking out of a stocking cap.

His diminutive cuteness, and his chosen sport, left Scott vulnerable to teasing by other boys. Although, as Hamilton would one day tell an interviewer, figure skating is an extremely athletic endeavor that demands the flexibility and strength of a gymnast and the stamina of a mile runner, this meant little to a preteen boy who was tired of being called a sissy. Scott Hamilton decided to join a hockey team, the Bowling Green Squirts.

Dorothy and Ernie realized they were not going to talk their pint-sized son out of going up against the bigger boys. They reluctantly let him play on the condition that he continue figure skating also. Scott actually turned out to be a pretty good offensive player because of his quick footwork, but he soon realized that his small size was a disadvantage. He later observed, "Speed and agility would get me to a certain level, but once I got to high school, I'd never be able to compete with the big guys." The signs of a troubled future in hockey were already there—especially when a friend on another team took him out so soundly that he spent two weeks in a neck brace!

Scott's hockey career lasted about three years, after which he decided to dedicate himself solely to figure skating.

Juggling two sports may have offered Scott a distraction from the disequilibrium that followed the departure of his first figure skating coach. Rita Lowery and her husband left the Bowling Green Skating Club in 1969. Before the Hamiltons found Scott's next coach, Italian-born Giuliano Grassi, Scott had struggled unsuccessfully to pass his first figures test. As Grassi's new charge, Scott passed the figure test in one try. However, the Hamiltons were not entirely happy with Grassi. His home rink was located in Fort Wayne, Indiana, so Scott spent every other weekend there. His coach came to Bowling Green the rest of the time. Although their son's skating was progressing, Ernie and Dorothy Hamilton felt that Grassi lacked the gentle touch that Scott needed. When they learned that he was also coaching a skater whom Scott frequently faced in competition, the Hamiltons decided that they no longer needed Giuliano Grassi's services.

His replacement was Herb Plata. Scott immediately took to Plata, a former German junior champion and professional show skater. Skater and coach got together during the 1970 season, forming an alliance that propelled Scott to the Juvenile men's title at the Eastern Great Lakes Regionals that year. This was significant because Regionals was the first stop on the road to the national championship: Regionals was followed by Sectionals, from which the champions from each section of the country (Eastern, Midwestern, and Pacific Coast) went to Nationals.

During the summer of 1970, Scott took his first long-distance competitive trip—to Culver City, California, for the Golden West Championships. Hamilton took second-place honors in freestyle skating and third in ice dancing in his group. Despite this success, the Golden West competition was the beginning of the end of Scott's ice-dancing career. Not only was it becoming increasingly difficult

to find partners of the right physical size, but he also needed to turn his full attention to solo skating.

By 1972, Scott Hamilton was approaching his goal of
national competition. He won the regional competition,
only to place fourth at Midwestern Sectionals. Fourth was
an impressive showing for someone who had been skating
for little more than four years, but the Hamiltons had a
decision to make. Dorothy and Ernie harbored doubts
about Scott's chances for continued improvement if he
stayed at Bowling Green with Herb Plata.

Dorothy Hamilton made some phone calls. She had
long provided the parental interest and hard work that
made her son's skating possible. Much of her salary, time,
and attention was consumed by Scott's practice and competitions. Yet, according to Scott and others who knew her,
Dorothy was not the stereotypical overbearing "skating
mother." As much as she and the rest of the family would
miss him, Dorothy believed that Scott needed to leave his
home ice to get more advanced coaching. The Hamiltons
sent Scott to train at the Wagon Wheel Resort in Rockton,
Illinois.

Dorothy originally wanted Slavka Kohout to coach her
son. Kohout had put the Wagon Wheel rink on the map of
great training facilities when she coached a young skater
named Janet Lynn to five national championship victories.
But Scott was placed in the hands of Pierre Brunet, a two-
time Olympic gold medalist in pairs skating who had been
coaching for over 25 years.

Despite an age difference of about 55 years, Monsieur
Brunet and Scott were a good fit. The new coach forced
Hamilton to pay close attention to his figures and to be
extremely mindful of his body's position on the ice.
Although figures training was difficult for a boy who
wanted to race, jump, and spin, such close concentration
would more than pay off in the future.

Scott started training in Rockton during the summer of
1972. For about a year, he shuttled between his home and

the Wagon Wheel, finally settling into a dormitory at the resort. Skating had taken him to a new full-time residence at the age of 15. This was not an easy adjustment for his parents, who were concerned because Scott was largely unsupervised. Dorothy Hamilton enlisted her daughter Sue to look out for Scott during his first extended stay at the Wagon Wheel. In the summer of 1972, Mrs. Hamilton gave Sue and her new husband a honeymoon at the resort as a wedding gift. When Sue's husband, who was in the U.S. Navy, was sent out to sea, Sue took a job at the Wagon Wheel for several more months—with a little encouragement from her mother.

Dorothy's worries were not entirely unfounded. Although the kids at Wagon Wheel trained hard for about six hours a day, they had a lot of unstructured time on their hands. They filled it with parties and practical jokes. Scott grew especially close to another one of Monsieur Brunet's pupils, Gordie McKellen. Gordie was about five years older than Scott—a Senior skater on the verge of winning his first national title—when he took on the task of mentoring the newcomer. With Gordie as his guide, Scott made his first tentative forays into adolescence: he discovered girls and joined in the general merriment at Wagon Wheel.

Such rites of passage didn't stop Hamilton from making Nationals as a Novice skater in 1972. He swept Regionals and Sectionals, only to finish ninth out of nine skaters at the National Championships in Minneapolis. Scott's friend Gordie emerged from the 1972 Nationals victorious, however. Though he still had far to go if he wanted to win a national title himself, Scott learned from Gordie McKellen how becoming a champion might affect his life.

Hamilton inched a little closer to the championship at the 1973 Nationals: this time, he placed ninth out of ten skaters. The 1974 season, however, would prove more frustrating: a severe injury to his right ankle kept Scott out of most major competitions that year. Ironically, he was hurt off the ice doing something mundane. He shattered the ankle while jumping out of the bunk in his dorm room at the Wagon Wheel. His quick return to the ice after the cast came off taught Scott how to skate through pain.

This injury was a setback for Scott's skating in 1974, but the news from home that year was even worse: Dorothy Hamilton was diagnosed with breast cancer. Although her illness and subsequent surgery and treatments slowed her down, she still taught at Bowling Green, and she saw Scott in competition whenever her strength permitted. Even though Dorothy's prognosis was uncertain, her belief that Scott's skating, and the sacrifices she had made to further it, were worthwhile remained steadfast. She would tell her friends that Scott was going to be an Olympian someday. "She never expressed that to me as much as she would to others," Scott later said of his mother's faith in him. "She was one of those who was proud and all that stuff."

Scott advanced to the Junior level in 1975, but this was a rare high point during an otherwise turbulent time in Scott's career. He qualified to compete at Nationals, which were held in Oakland, California. Pierre Brunet's emphasis on figures paid off; Scott made a strong showing in the compulsory figures segment of the competition. His short program was also good. It was the long program that bogged Hamilton down. As a boy, he had wanted to jump and spin unfettered; as a young man, the freestyle segment seemed to shake his confidence. Scott's rattled nerves left him out of the medals with a seventh-place finish.

After the 1975 Nationals, Monsieur Brunet retired, leaving Scott without a coach once more. Mary Ludington, who had been a choreographer at the Wagon Wheel, was soon joined by a new coach named Evy Scotvold. The pair, who would later marry and co-coach greats like Nancy Kerrigan and Paul Wylie, helped Scott get ready for the 1976 season. The Scotvolds would also coach David Santee, one of Hamilton's chief rivals during the early 1980s.

Also absent after 1975 was the stabilizing presence of Gordie McKellen, who retired from amateur competition after winning three national championships.

As if these changes weren't enough to face, the Hamilton family had run out of money to finance Scott's skating. The 1976 season would be his last chance to make his mark at Nationals. Taking this fact to heart, Scott won Regionals and Midwesterns: he also sadly resigned himself to hanging up his skates and starting his freshman year at Bowling Green State University in the coming fall.

Scott's climb to the top had not gone unnoticed, though, and a coach named Carlo Fassi decided to reward his efforts. Working with his wife, Christa, he was fast becoming a living legend among figure skating coaches: two of Fassi's students, John Curry and Dorothy Hamill, won Olympic gold in 1976. Acting as an intermediary, Carlo Fassi connected the Hamiltons with a wealthy couple who enjoyed supporting the efforts of young figure skaters. His new benefactors would ultimately contribute, in Scott's estimation, "six figures" to the continuation of his career. Fassi urged the Hamiltons to keep the arrangement a secret from their son until after Nationals.

Meanwhile, at the 1976 National Championships in Colorado Springs, Colorado, Scott skated as if this competition was indeed his last. He was in a position to win after figures and the short program. But, believing that his amateur skating career was ending, he was practically inconsolable on the night of the long program. Dorothy, who did not want her son to skate with a heavy heart, spilled the wonderful secret before Scott took the ice.

Dorothy Hamilton's decision to tell the him the news was a good one: Scott's long program clinched the United States Junior championship. On his way home from Nationals, Scott stopped in Winnetka, Illinois, to meet the couple who was funding his dream and thank them in person.

In an interview with *Sports Illustrated* magazine before

*Well-known skating coach Carlo Fassi connected Hamilton with a wealthy couple who paid the expenses of his training, enabling Hamilton to continue working toward success as an amateur skater.*

the 1984 Olympics, Hamilton explained that his benefactors did much more than simply fund his efforts. "They became like a second set of parents," he said, "insisting that I develop my character and responsibility as well as my skating."

Generous as the couple's gift was, it was not unconditional. Scott would become Carlo Fassi's student, which necessitated a move to Denver for training at the Colorado Ice Arena. In Denver, Scott took up residence with the local family that had housed Dorothy Hamill when she was training with Fassi; in fact, he stayed in Hamill's former room. Hamilton formed a warm relationship with the family.

This setup probably contributed to his graduating from high school on time. He attended a local high school and arranged to take some correspondence courses from Bowling Green's high school. Since he had lost a lot of class time over the years, particularly during his stay at the Wagon Wheel, Scott had to cram in order to don cap and gown at commencement exercises in Bowling Green that spring.

In the summer, Scott passed his last figures test, enabling him to compete as a Senior at last. He also tried his wings off of the ice, acquiring his own car and renting an apartment near the Colorado Ice Arena. As 1976 was drawing to a close, Scott's life seemed to be opening up to new possibilities. For the first time, skating had become a means to a greater goal, rather than just something that Hamilton loved to do.

"In 1976 I won the Junior National Championship and I thought, 'Whoa, I might get pretty good at this!'" he later recalled. "And then I'm thinking, 'Well, four years away, maybe the Olympics are possible.'"

Hamilton's hunch was right, but several obstacles still awaited him.

*The intense concentration necessary to succeed at competitive figure skating is obvious in Scott Hamilton's face as he completes a jump during the 1982 U.S. National Championships.*

# 4

# SKATING TO THE TOP

INJURY SOMEWHAT DAMPENED Scott Hamilton's sense of what was possible in 1977. He had to sit out Regionals that year, but he made it back to the ice in time to skate at Sectionals. His third-place finish was disappointing, but still good enough for a place in the national competition. During Olympic years, the top senior-level finishers at Nationals advance to the Games. But in 1977, Scott Hamilton was in no position to even speculate on his Olympic future. He placed ninth—a place that at times seemed to be reserved exclusively for him—at the 1977 Nationals.

That was the last competition Dorothy Hamilton felt well enough to attend. The less-than-glorious outcome saddened Scott because he longed to make his mother proud. She saw him skate in one more exhibition, and Ernie showed her a videotaped portion of Bowling Green Skating Club's 1977 Ice Horizons show. By then, however, she was so

*After the death of his mother, Dorothy, in 1977, Hamilton devoted greater attention to his skating. His hard work, along with switching to a new coach, Don Laws, paid off as he made steady improvement on the national figure skating scene, culminating in a third-place finish at the 1980 U.S. National Championships that earned him a spot on the United States' team for the 1980 Winter Olympics.*

exhausted by her long fight with cancer that even watching a tape from her hospital bed proved too much for her.

The end finally came for Dorothy Hamilton on May 19, 1977. Scott visited her at the hospital with his brother Steve on the last night of her life. Dorothy's death shattered Scott. When his grief was still fresh, he sat beside the backyard pond of his family's home and spoke to no one. This was a make-or-break juncture in Hamilton's career. Would he crumble and skate poorly in his grief?

Hamilton has said that he skated his way out of the illness that once threatened his own future: when his mother died, he recommitted himself to skating. In *Pat Summerall's Sports in America*, Scott recalled how his mother's death led to his transformation into a hungry competitor:

> [W]hen she died, a lot of my lack of focus disappeared, because she really worked hard to keep me in my skating. She did a lot of work and had a lot of heartache and a lot of pain. She suffered a lot trying to get more work and bet-

ter work to pay for my skating when she was suffering from cancer. I didn't want everything she went through to be wasted because I was lazy or because I wasn't focused.

Scott's renewed discipline reaped measurable results in the 1978 season. Not only did he earn his first medal at Nationals with a third-place finish, but he also made a fine showing in his first World Championships. Hamilton placed 11th at the competition, which took place in Ottawa, Canada. His emergence onto the international figure skating scene represented a dramatic improvement over the course of a single year.

Scott Hamilton's new course was not always a steady one, though. The next season saw him hampered by an injured right ankle. Hamilton's confidence also took a blow when he learned that Carlo Fassi had agreed to coach Scott Cramer, one of his competitors. He finished out of the medals at Nationals in 1979. Scott Hamilton had planned on skating with the U.S. team in Vienna, Austria, that year; instead, he wound up watching the World Championships on TV at home.

Determined not to let that happen again in 1980, he made some changes. He ended his relationship with Carlo Fassi. His future up in the air, Hamilton relocated again: this time to Ardmore, Pennsylvania, and the Philadelphia Skating Club and Humane Society rink, where he teamed up with a little-known coach named Don Laws. The dapper, silver-haired Laws did something that nobody had since Pierre Brunet retired: he won the skater's complete trust and confidence.

Their collaboration gave birth to the Wow-Wow-Wow Theory of competition skating. "We've got to play on emotions," Don Laws explained. "Show them excitement, hazard. Give them 45 seconds of downright dangerous stuff and then throw in some whimsy."

Most of Hamilton's days were consumed by his demanding practices with Laws. His serious regimen and new coach paid off almost immediately. In a matter of

*Hamilton, the smallest member of the 1980 U.S. Olympic team, was asked to lead the team into the opening ceremony of the Winter Games carrying the American flag. With him in this photo is U.S. speed skater Eric Heiden, who won a record five gold medals in the 1980 Olympics. Although Hamilton would not win a medal at the Lake Placid Games, he later remarked that in some ways, he enjoyed the 1980 Games more than the 1984 Winter Olympics.*

months, Scott won his first international competition. He surprised more than a few skating fans with his victory in the Flaming Leaves competition (now SkateAmerica) in Lake Placid, New York. Because his Flaming Leaves win came in the fall of 1979, Hamilton was suddenly regarded as an especially strong contender for a spot on the 1980 Olympic team.

He lived up to his newfound reputation in January 1980, with a third-place showing in Nationals. Charlie Tickner

won; Hamilton finished behind David Santee. Third place
was good enough for a trip back to Lake Placid for the
1980 Winter Olympic Games.

He did not go to these Games with visions of gold dancing in his head; all Hamilton wanted at first was to end up
in the top 10. Once he got to Lake Placid, however, he
upped the ante. His new goal was to finish in the top five.
Although Hamilton was nervous, he realized that his
performance would not be burdened with the world's
expectations for a gold-medal finish. The only standards
he really had to meet this time were his own. He has since
said that in some ways he enjoyed the 1980 Winter Games
even more than the 1984 Olympics.

Romance was probably a major contributor to Hamilton's fond memories of the Lake Placid Olympics. He was
dating another Olympic team member, pairs skater Caitlin
"Kitty" Carruthers, whose partner was her brother, Peter.
(Kitty and Peter Carruthers would go on to win a silver
medal in the 1984 Olympics.) Scott and Kitty savored the
excitement of their first Olympics together. He had met his
girlfriend after moving to Philadelphia in 1979. Scott
became fast friends with both of the Carrutherses, who
trained in nearby Wilmington, Delaware. His and Kitty's
relationship would be an on-and-off affair. To Hamilton's
chagrin, the relationship would eventually fall prey to the
pressures of competitive figure skating—the very thing
that first brought them together.

At the opening ceremonies in Lake Placid, Scott Hamilton was chosen to carry the American flag. "The team had
a meeting about who to pick," he later recalled, "and
someone made this emotional pitch for me, pointing out
that I had overcome terrible obstacles, sickness and all,
and that my mom had died at a crucial point in my career,
and that I was the smallest male Olympian there." The
oversized cowboy hat that completed his uniform may
have obscured his smiling face, but nothing could dimin-
ish his stature in the eyes of the world as he led the Unit-

ed States Olympic team into the stadium.

Hamilton's performance at the 1980 Olympics would prove another source of pride. He placed fifth, right behind David Santee. His long program, featuring six clean triple jumps, was his brightest moment at Lake Placid. He followed up the Olympics with another fifth-place finish at the 1980 Worlds competition in March.

Although Scott Hamilton's best skating was still to come, Bowling Green honored its hometown figure skating hero along with two other local Olympians who had played on the triumphant United States hockey team. When spring came, he skated in the Bowling Green Skating Club's ice show. This time, Scott had a greater personal investment in the show than ever before: he skated to raise funds for the American Cancer Society in memory of his mother. The Bowling Green rink would continue to host an American Cancer Society benefit every other year, alternating with the Ice Horizons show.

Hamilton had forged a productive relationship with his coach, but Don Laws was headed to Denver for a post at the Colorado Ice Arena. Scott's decision to follow Laws back to Denver was music to the ears of the Landis family, with whom he had stayed just a few years earlier while training with Carlo Fassi. Scott was particularly close with the Landises' son. His old room was waiting for him, and he happily took it.

His 1980 Olympic performance had placed Scott Hamilton on the map as a strong medal contender for 1984. His growing fame brought increased pressure to perform. The 1981 Nationals would be a proving ground for Hamilton. Charlie Tickner, the 1980 national champion, had turned professional, leaving Hamilton and David Santee embattled for the top spot on the medals podium. The figures and short program section of the 1981 Nationals found both skaters in strong positions.

Scott's prospects were good when tragedy threatened to revisit the Hamilton family. Ernie, Scott's number-one

supporter since Dorothy's death, had accompanied his son to the championships in San Diego, California. He harbored a potentially deadly secret for most of the competition, though. Numbness crept into Ernie Hamilton's left arm on the day of Scott's short program, rendering it almost useless. He immediately realized that he had suffered a mild stroke.

But Dr. Hamilton's response to this emergency was less than immediate. He kept his stroke a secret until after Scott had completed his long program some two days later! "I couldn't tell Scotty because this was his big chance," the elder Hamilton later recalled:

> My friends knew what had happened and they were worried. So was I. On the day of the men's finals, I went over

*Hamilton went into the 1980 Olympics as the third member of the U.S. team. His goal entering the competition was to finish in the top 10; at the Games, however, he showed that he was a rising force in international skating with a strong fifth-place finish.*

to the arena and talked to Scotty, to assure him that I loved him no matter what. I deliberately kept turned away from him so that my left arm and hand wouldn't show. And I spoke slowly, enunciating my words as best I could. He was so excited about the competition that somehow I got by with it.

After wishing Scott luck before his long program, Ernie Hamilton quietly checked into a hospital.

It is not surprising that Scott was too preoccupied to see through Ernie's attempt to hide his condition. David Santee's brilliant performance in the long program commanded his full attention. Santee skated to music from the 1979 motion picture *Rocky*. "Rocky" Santee landed six triple jumps, exhibited neat footwork, and executed powerful spins.

David Santee was so good that there would have been no shame in finishing second to him. But Scott Hamilton had other plans. Although his program included only five triple jumps to Santee's six, Hamilton made every element count. His jumps were clean; his footwork, precise and just short of hazardous (per the Wow-Wow-Wow Theory). He wrapped up his performance with a dazzling, blurring spin that had scarcely slowed before the crowd was on its feet.

Scott's skating captivated judges and fans alike. Hamilton received his first perfect marks in competition from two judges for artistic merit. In national- and international-level figure skating competitions, a panel of nine judges awards each skater two marks: one for technical merit and one for artistic merit. These marks range from 0.0 for a performance not skated to 6.0 for a perfect showing. Each judge's pair of scores is combined, and the total is called the ordinal mark. Each judge's ordinal is then compared with those awarded by the rest of the judges. To win the short program, for example, a skater must be awarded more first-place ordinals than any of the other contestants in that event.

*Hamilton is congratulated by coach Don Laws after winning the world championship in 1981. In one year, the diminutive skater improved from his fifth-place finish at the Olympics and World Championships to become the best skater in the world.*

Hamilton was the only skater at Nationals to get a 6.0 during any phase of the competition. No longer would Scott Hamilton trail behind David Santee, who had to settle for a silver medal that night.

Dr. Hamilton's friends helped keep up the subterfuge until Scott successfully completed his skate. Whenever Scott would ask about his father's whereabouts, the other members of the Hamilton camp fibbed that they had just seen him. Ernie, meanwhile, had refused to let hospital personnel sedate him until he watched Scott win on TV and then saw the new national champion in person. When Scott learned about his father's stroke, he rushed to Ernie's

hospital room. Finally, at around one o'clock in the morning, the devoted father allowed medical treatment to begin:
"O.K. guys, you can put me under now," Ernie said.

Ernie's refusal to disclose his stroke may have helped
his son attain the 1981 national title, but it also threatened
his health. Although Dr. Hamilton eventually recovered,
Scott was sufficiently worried to consider skipping the
upcoming World Championships. With his father's
encouragement, however, Scott headed off to Hartford,
Connecticut, and the competition.

As expected, Hamilton and Santee were again in close
competition. Scott advanced from fourth after figures to
third after his short program; David Santee led the pack
after the short program. The long program highlighted
Scott Hamilton's personal magic. He fell during footwork
but more than compensated for this single mistake with a
vigorous, enthralling presentation on the ice. His technical
marks were only slightly lower than his sterling artistic
scores. David Santee could not hold onto his lead in light
of a performance like Scott's. He made only one mistake
on a jump, but wound up with the silver medal because his
performance lacked the astonishing expressiveness of
Hamilton's winning effort.

In just one year, Scott Hamilton had catapulted from a
fifth-place finish at the Olympics to the world championship. No trace remained of the nervous, aimless young
skater Scott claimed to have been prior to his mother's
death. Now he would need all of the single-mindedness he
could muster to cope with the pressures that accompanied
being the best in the world.

Scott was in the media's eye and frequently displayed
great intelligence and wit during interviews in which he
discussed his own skating. When the top brass at CBS
Sports heard his humorous, insightful remarks, they decided that it was time for Hamilton to try his hand at commentary.

Although he would eventually tell *International Figure*

*Skating* magazine, "I love talking about people's skating," Scott found his early attempts at commentary difficult at best. He would become tense and intimidated when paired with more experienced broadcasters. Furthermore, Hamilton sometimes wondered why he was bothering with commentary when he still had years of amateur competition ahead of him. He rationalized it as a way of launching a second career before his skating days were over. But then again, didn't he have a reputation to uphold as the world champion of men's figure skating? Scott often wondered if pursuits like TV commentary were worthwhile when there was so much training to do to stay on top.

Suddenly there never seemed to be enough time. He couldn't have a practice skate at competitions without being pursued by the press. Agents courted him relentlessly. Ironically, now that the world championship was his Scott Hamilton felt more self-doubt than ever. How was he supposed to defend his title when it came with so many potential distractions?

"I demanded so much more out of myself that for awhile I became a basket case," he later admitted. "I was harsh and demanding on the people around me. I had a great relationship with a girlfriend and I turned that into a weird thing." It was during the difficult 1982 competitive season that Michael Steere, a newspaper staff writer for the *Toledo Blade*, turned on his tape recorder and went on the road with Hamilton, gathering interviews, eyewitness accounts, and information for a biography.

Although skating as the defending world champion temporarily dulled Hamilton's sense of joy, his skating remained unspoiled. This was fortunate, because the 1982 National Men's Figure Skating Championships featured a closely matched pack of competitors. David Santee was there, of course, but so were two gifted skaters named Robert Wagenhoffer and Mark Cockerell. Another medal contender named Brian Boitano was also present for his first Nationals.

*The pressure was on Hamilton in 1982 to retain his national and world championship titles; he responded with strong performances to win both competitions. As he mastered the technical aspects of his sport, Hamilton was also developing an expressive skating style unlike that of past champions: he incorporated humor and crowd-pleasing elements into his programs.*

When Scott took the ice in Indianapolis, Indiana, for the figures segment, he bobbled slightly on a particularly difficult type of figure called a paragraph double three. This figure required the skater to lay out and trace two circles on the ice and repeat the pattern five more times. Michael Steere described the technical demands of the paragraph double three this way: ". . . the skater has to turn around twice in each circle. He begins each going forward, then turns and glides backward through a third of each circle. Two-thirds of the way through each circle, the skater must turn around again, and return to the figure's center going forward."

Hamilton kept his composure and asked for a chance to repeat the botched figure, pointing to a problem spot on his patch of ice. The judges agreed that his trouble had stemmed from bad ice, and Scott skated the paragraph double three again—this time, without a hitch.

In the short program, however, Scott had only himself to blame for a missed double axel. He fell on this relatively easy jump and was visibly disappointed in himself after his skate.

Hamilton needed a stellar long program to clinch the national championship. He came through, probably aided by the misfortune of David Santee, who skated to third place overall with a painful groin injury. Robert Wagenhoffer, a tremendously talented skater who lacked Scott's work ethic, finished second. Young Brian Boitano's long program clearly demonstrated that he was next in line for stardom, but he ended up in fourth place overall.

Hamilton's performance at the 1982 World Championships in Copenhagen, Denmark, was not marred by bad ice, missed double axels, or anything else. So soundly did he sweep the figures and the short program that he did not have to win his long program to take the gold.

More than ever, Hamilton could afford to take risks in the freeskate. He took a gamble in the form of the "futzy" section of his long program, so nicknamed because Hamilton "futzed around" on the ice. He and Laws had selected an interlude of classical music (from the ballet *Sylvia* by 19th century French composer Leo Delibes) that was instantly recognizable because it had often been spoofed in cartoons. When this music played in his program, Scott flashed a quizzical face, shrugged, then pranced across the ice in a bit of lighthearted self-parody. This was riskier than it sounds, because no one had ever attempted to test the judges' reaction to humor in competition.

The risk apparently paid off. The 1981 world champion retained his crown in 1982.

The success of the humorous content in Scott Hamilton's programs boded well for him. He was learning that not only could he succeed in men's figure skating, he could also influence the sport. One of Hamilton's main

*Hamilton glides into the lead at the 1983 U.S. National Championships in Pittsburgh. A few weeks later, he became the first skater in 24 years to win the World Championships in three consecutive years.*

concerns was the image of figure skating. "At the end of a performance, people shouldn't swoon," he said before the 1984 Olympics. "They should look upon it as a sporting event."

He believed that figure skaters, particularly Europeans, borrowed too much from ballet and dance in terms of choreography and costumes. "If I'm showing strength and angular positions, and if I'm connecting each step with positions that aren't really based on ballet or jazz, it adds to the intensity and the drama of the performance as well as trying to create a masculine look," Hamilton said in *Pat Sumerall's Sports in America.*

Hamilton's efforts to create a masculine, athletic style of skating went beyond the straightforward choreography that he called "apple pies and Chevrolets." In 1983, he turned his attention to his costumes. He won the 1983 National Championships in Pittsburgh, Pennsylvania, wearing a light blue costume with a sprinkling of sequins across the chest, the same outfit he'd worn to clinch his two previous national titles. But Hamilton wanted others to see him as he saw himself: as an athlete taking part in a sport. Too often, he thought, male skaters bedecked themselves with sequins and beads in the hope of favorably impressing the judges. "Pretty soon we were going to have to wear push up dresses and bustles," Hamilton later remarked.

He unveiled his sartorial reaction to all those sparkles at the 1983 Worlds in Helsinki, Finland. The two-time defending world champion wore a stretch suit similar to those worn by speed skaters. It was a sleek, black, one-piece outfit with a white stripe running down the sleeves. Hamilton said just wearing it gave him an added psychological boost. "It feels like a million bucks," said the young man who had grudgingly worn sequined costumes for more than a dozen years.

The un-glimmering Scott Hamilton placed second in figures at the World Championships, but won both the short and long programs, making his third consecutive victory a definitive one. With the 1983 world championship, Scott Hamilton became the first figure skater in 24 years to win three consecutive world titles. The last three-time champ, fellow American David Jenkins (who won from 1957–59), was now an admirer of Scott's skating.

Hamilton's only source of consternation in Helsinki was his continued inability to land a triple flip (one leg extended straight back while leaping from the other foot, rotating three times in the air, and landing on the opposite

*The eyes of the skating world were on Scott Hamilton after he won his fourth consecutive national title in January 1984. The 25-year-old was favored to take gold in the '84 Winter Olympics in Sarajevo, Yugoslavia.*

foot) in competition. In 1984, he would need the triple flip in his arsenal more than ever. The International Skating Union (ISU) had just instituted a new rule that skaters could not do the same triple jump twice in one program unless the second jump was part of a combination. Hamilton's friend, 1982 ladies' world champion Elaine Zayak, had unwittingly inspired the rule with her tendency to repeat certain jumps several times in her long programs. Scott needed to add the triple flip to his old repertoire (triple lutz, triple toe loop, triple salchow) in order to give the judges and the audience sufficient variety.

Hamilton's long program for the 1984 National Championships took this new rule into account. The competition was held in Salt Lake City, Utah. Twenty-five-year-old Scott Hamilton wore one of his new trademark suits—blue with a red stripe spanning the sleeves and chest—as he skated onto the ice.

The triple flip was his second planned jump. He usually popped it into a double jump. But this time Hamilton held onto it, landing on one foot after three full rotations in the air! By nailing the difficult jump, Hamilton knew he was virtually assured of his fourth national title in as many years, and could afford to skate with his customary exuberance. He sailed through four minutes of intricate footwork and triple-double jump combinations into a blurring spin that signaled the end of his skate. Smiling broadly, Hamilton drank in his well-earned standing ovation. He was rewarded again when his marks were tallied—with four artistic marks of 6.0.

The Nationals win was his ticket to the 1984 Olympic Games in Sarajevo, Yugoslavia. Even before Nationals, most people had taken it for granted that Scott Hamilton was headed to the 1984 Winter Olympics as America's leading gold-medal contender, but he had outdone himself in Salt Lake City. Could Hamilton maintain the incredible momentum he had built up over the past four years? Would it propel him to the top of the medals podium at Sarajevo?

The nation's best skater harbored some private doubts.

*Scott Hamilton has tears in his eyes as the "Star-Spangled Banner" is played, marking his gold-medal victory in the 1984 Olympics. With him on the medals podium are silver-medal winner Brian Orser of Canada and bronze winner Josef Sabovcik of Czechoslovakia.*

# 5

# STRIKING GOLD

AN OLYMPIC GOLD MEDAL was the only award missing from Scott Hamilton's collection when he headed for Sarajevo, a major city in the region of Yugoslavia that is now the republic of Bosnia-Herce-govina. Hamilton fans who had spent the past four years watching him win everything in sight felt increasing affection for their champion with every triumph. Their reasons went beyond the clichéd observation that everyone loves a winner. He had a winning way off the ice, too.

Hamilton's politeness and self-deprecating humor were evident whenever he faced questions from the press about his size. "Once I bought a tuxedo, and when I got it home, I discovered the hole in the back of the jacket where the ventriloquist puts his hand," he would say in mock agreement with reporters who expressed wonder at how small he was. There were other well-rehearsed comebacks, too, but the diminutive skater never lost his cool.

*Hamilton carefully cuts a design in the ice during the compulsory figures segment of the 1984 Olympic competition. Hamilton led all skaters after the figures segment was complete; that lead would ultimately be enough for him to hang on for the gold, as his skating performances during his long and short programs were hampered by an ear infection that affected his balance on the ice.*

He needed at least to appear oblivious to the unspoken pressure to deliver the performance of his life at the Olympics. The source of this pressure was both internal and external. The bittersweet paradox of being a skating champion is that talent and drive take the athlete to the pinnacle of the sport, but each time the athlete performs brilliantly, people immediately expect more. There had to be a ceiling to his achievements, Hamilton reasoned. He feared that he would not be able to top himself as all of America watched.

To escape some of his external pressures, Hamilton spent a week in Paris, fine-tuning his figures and routines away from the relentless press coverage that awaited him in Sarajevo. The practices went well.

As he prepared for his date with destiny in Sarajevo, however, Hamilton caught a cold. This in itself was not unmanageable. But when the cold led to an ear infection, both skater and coach became concerned. They knew that an ear infection could affect Hamilton's balance and his orientation on the ice. Scott did not want this to be a factor in anyone's evaluation of his Olympic performance, so he kept his health status to himself until the men's figure skating events were over.

After participating in the opening ceremonies of the 1984 Winter Olympic Games, Hamilton had to wait for over a week for his event to begin. He filled 90 minutes of each day with practice sessions at Sarajevo's Zetra Arena. Each skater was allotted the same amount of ice time, but Scott Hamilton had more interferences to cope with than any of his peers. Reporters and photographers followed him wherever he went, including to practices.

Later, he would reflect on the difficulties he faced at the 1984 Olympics. "It's hard to be the guy everybody has on his or her list to interview," he observed.

One of the press's favorite topics was Scott's childhood illness and his resulting small size. *Newsweek* gave the matter tongue-in-cheek treatment, with an article entitled "Great Scott Won't Be Sold Short" in its Olympic preview section. In the piece, Hamilton confidently told his interviewer, "There's no one who's competing that has ever beaten me before." But inwardly, he was more than a little afraid that he might somehow miss capping his amateur career with the gold medal that seemed to be his for the taking.

In addition to the specter of self-doubt and the glare of publicity, Scott Hamilton faced the same ordeal that jangled the nerves of all competitive figure skaters. Skating competitions are not day-long contests in which everyone skates once. Rather, they consist of three events in distinct skill areas, and they last for several days.

The first event was compulsory figures (the USFSA eliminated the figures segment from competition in 1990). In the 1984 Olympics, a skater's execution of three different figures would be worth 30 percent of his or her overall score. Because they counted so heavily, compulsory figures were the downfall of many gifted freeskaters who had never taken the time to master the painstaking practice of etching precise figures on a patch of ice.

Pierre Brunet's exhaustive figures work with his teenage pupil would pay off in Sarajevo. Hamilton typically finished figures in second or third place, then relied on his musicality and skill in the long program to sew up a victory. This time, though, he buckled down and earned top marks in all three of the required figures. Scott Hamilton would ultimately need his lead in figures more than he could imagine at this point in the competition.

The short, or technical, program was next, weighing in at 20 percent of the total score. This tension-filled exercise was a two-minute routine that had to incorporate seven required elements: a combination jump, a double axel, a double flip, footwork, a sit spin (a spin on one foot, in sitting position on the ice), a forward camel spin, and a combination spin. Theoretically, each skater had a perfect score going into the program; deductions followed each missed or flawed element.

Hamilton, known for the blurring speed of his spins, could not get his sit spin or his forward camel spin going. Neither was up to his usual standards. His footwork was fleet but uncontrolled. The ear infection had not yet cleared, and it may have contributed to his difficulties in the short program. Although he seemed upset by his performance, Hamilton placed second and was still in a strong position to win at the end of the short program.

The only skater to beat him in this section of the com-

*To the cheers of the crowd at Sarajevo's Zetra Arena, Hamilton skates with the American flag the night of his gold-medal victory, February 16, 1984.*

petition was Canada's Brian Orser. Orser was a lyrical, graceful skater who shared Scott's extraordinary ability to interpret music. He differed in that he lacked Hamilton's jaunty athleticism and his skill in figures. In fact, Orser had scored so low in the figures segment that only a truly disastrous freeskate by Hamilton would pave the way for him to win.

"There's a big difference between going to the Olympics and going to the Olympics to win," Hamilton later told interviewer Pat Summerall. At no point in the 1984 games did this appear more true than during the men's figure skating long program. Hamilton skated after Brian Orser, who had landed a clean triple axel for a total of six triple jumps in his routine. Scott's repertoire didn't include the triple axel. One jump he thought he had finally conquered—the triple flip—abandoned him, too. Hamilton popped it into a single! A planned triple salchow withered into a double. But Hamilton's ability to maintain his composure without letting a sense of disaster overwhelm him was a mark of his maturity. He held on to skate very well overall, diminishing the difficulty of the program only by botching the two jumps and moving a bit more slowly than usual. The smiling, ebullient presence that made Hamilton who he was on the ice was markedly subdued, however.

When his four-and-a-half minute long program was over, Hamilton was seen mouthing the words "I'm sorry," to Don Laws.

As it turned out, no apologies were necessary. Brian Orser took the long program, but Scott Hamilton won overall. It was not the skate of his life, but it was a performance to be proud of nonetheless. He had his Olympic gold medal; he pronounced silver medalist Orser "great." Years later, Orser would be on hand to help celebrate Hamilton's first postcancer ice show.

He stepped to the top of the medals podium, flanked by Brian Orser and the bronze medalist, Hungary's Josef Sabovcik. Years of elation and disappointment, privilege and sacrifice, had built up inside of Scott Hamilton—all leading up to this moment. His eyes welled with tears as he listened to "The Star-Spangled Banner" reverberate through Zetra Arena.

"A lot of people really get emotionally involved in the games, and I think it's to be shared," the gold medalist later reflected. "If I would've had a disastrous performance at the Olympic Games, it would've been really difficult for me to live with because I would've felt like I let down a lot of people."

At just 25 years of age, Scott Hamilton had reached the pinnacle of his career. He had been on the job for over 15 years—longer than many nonathletes stick with a single profession. His life of crowd-pleasing was by no means over, though.

*Scott Hamilton proudly displays an award from the Philadelphia Sports Writers Association honoring him as "Most Courageous Athlete of 1984." After following his Olympic gold with his fourth consecutive world figure skating championship, Hamilton decided to retire from amateur figure skating.*

# 6

# JOB HUNTING

SCOTT HAMILTON'S ROAD to Sarajevo had been paved with sacrifice. Spending as many as 20 hours a week on the ice while still in elementary school, he had gladly forfeited what many people would describe as a "normal" childhood—regular school hours, and weekends at home with family and friends. But Hamilton's unconventional upbringing seemed to have suited him marvelously. He benefited physically from skating, his confidence soared, and his athletic achievements opened doors to possible second careers such as broadcasting or coaching.

He had yet to reap financial rewards from skating, though. Current amateur rules allow skaters to participate in USFSA-sanctioned competitions and collect substantial sums of prize money. Nonprofessional athletes can also endorse products. These enterprises allow them to train without drowning in the expense of an amateur career. Coaching, for instance, carries a staggering price tag. *Sports Illustrated* quoted Don Laws's hourly rate to train Scott for the 1984 Olympics at $45. Inflate this figure to 1998 dollars, and it becomes clear that most top

*Scott enjoyed many post-Olympic celebrations, including a parade through downtown Denver, where he had trained for the Games, and the naming of a street in his honor in his hometown of Bowling Green.*

amateur skaters and their families would go bankrupt without opportunities to make money as they strive for Olympic glory.

In 1984, however, amateurs were forbidden from making money in competitions or through endorsements. Scott Hamilton relied on his benefactor, whose husband had died, to cover his training costs, and he was living a no-frills existence off the ice. The proceeds from a few pinball machines at the Colorado Ice Arena provided him with pocket money. He had invested in the machines with Don Laws as a means of earning money without violating USFSA rules or cutting into valuable training time.

Although after the Olympics Hamilton was eager to embark on a life less dictated by training and competition

schedules, he wanted to stick around long enough for the 1984 World Championships in Ottawa. Although his main rival, Brian Orser, later said that Scott was a less-than-interested presence at Worlds, Hamilton retained his title. He won the figures by a wide margin, then skated a short program that further bolstered his first-place standing. Hamilton wrapped up his fourth world championship with a fine long program. All in all, his performance surpassed his Olympic skate of just one month earlier. It was a praiseworthy close to an incredible amateur career.

After this championship, it was generally assumed that Hamilton would retire from amateur figure skating. He had wisely avoided signing with any of the agents who had wooed him over the years. With 18 consecutive gold medals under his belt, Hamilton knew that his name and face were now worth a great deal; signing with an agent earlier would have limited his earning potential.

On March 29, 1984, Hamilton announced his retirement from amateur figure skating. He told the crowd gathered at his press conference in Atlantic City, New Jersey, that he needed to "go on to the adult part of [his] life." Agents at International Management Group (IMG) would represent Scott Hamilton.

He did not immediately leap into the life of a touring ice pro, however. In May, Hamilton made a triumphant return visit to Bowling Green, where a street was now named after him. That visit was just one episode in a spring season that had already included a parade for him in Denver and a visit with President Ronald Reagan at the White House. Although he wasn't absolutely sure what he was going to do with his life, Hamilton definitely enjoyed speaking at Bowling Green–area schools, where he answered questions posed by adoring grade-schoolers.

There was one more thing to do in Bowling Green. On the same ice where he once tried his first faltering jumps and spins, Scott Hamilton gave his final amateur performance. He was joined by other friends who were ending their amateur careers: 1983 world champion Rosalynn Sumners, and Peter and Kitty Carruthers. Scott gratefully acknowledged donations to the Dorothy Hamilton Memorial Fund, and his program was a special tribute to his mother. Michael Steere closed his biography of Hamilton with a stirring description of the Olympic champion standing center ice at the end of his last amateur performance:

> He drew down the zipper of his skating costume, from collar to heart level, and fished up a ribbon from which hung a shining disk of gold. He was showing the people the Olympic gold wrought from the ice in front of them, where a little boy, supposedly dying, had started skating eighteen years earlier. . . .
>
> But it seemed to me just then, as it seemed to other

Scott people, that Scott Hamilton was not showing the medal to us. No, he was showing it to Dorothy Hamilton, who had always known that the gold medal belonged to her son.

When he got back to Denver, Hamilton began living on his own for the first time since he was 19 years old. He also started a brief stint on the coaching staff of the Colorado Ice Arena while he contemplated his future in skating. "The parents drove me a little crazy but I liked the kids a lot," Hamilton later said of his coaching experience.

In the summer of 1984, Scott put his coaching days behind him and signed on with the Ice Capades. Although he no longer had to etch precise figures into the ice on demand, Hamilton found that professional skating had grueling aspects all its own. He was often expected to skate in more than one show per day. His existence became almost nomadic as the Ice Capades moved from city to city.

Then there was the matter of Hamilton's costars: not all

*After a brief stint as a coach, Hamilton returned to his first love, figure skating, as a professional with the Ice Capades. Although he enjoyed his time with the traveling ice show, he hoped that someday he could be part of a professional ice tour where the performers continued to strive for improvement in their routines.*

of them were people. Some costumed cartoon characters were also on the bill. The transition from competition—which he later described as "a very egocentric environment"—to being part of a touring company was a challenging one. "When you're in an ice show you're a 'star,'" he told *American Skating World* in 1987, "but also just a piece of a big machine. It's a big adjustment. . . . You never really get the strokes you did when you were an amateur."

Ice shows were sometimes looked upon as places where once-dedicated champions cashed in on their skating before their skills eroded. Professional skating generally included little artistic experimentation. Rather than pushing to acquire new athletic skills, many ice pros just tried to keep in good-enough shape to maintain their old techniques.

Scott Hamilton wanted his future to be different. Although he recognized serious figure skating as "a great destroyer of bodies," and understood that he probably wouldn't be landing triple jumps as an 80-year-old, he was not content to stop growing just because he had made the switch from amateur athlete to paid entertainer. He added the backflip to his bag of tricks with the help of 1964 Olympic gymnast Greg Weiss (who is also the father of 1998 Olympic figure skater Michael Weiss).

"In professional skating, there's a lot of flipping," Hamilton later explained. "For that you need harnesses, you need spotters, you need a lot of off-the-ice training in order to learn . . . . [W]ith gymnastic moves like back-flips and things like that, you really can learn off the ice. And you're better to learn them off the ice then take them on the ice, because of the danger involved in going heels over head."

Greg Weiss worked with Hamilton over the course of one weekend, spotting him as he backflipped first on the floor, then on the ice. Weiss remembered Hamilton as a quick study who got the hang of the backflip after about 30 attempts on the floor; in Weiss's estimation it takes most people at least 100 tries to reach that point.

As he added a guaranteed crowd-pleaser to his repertoire, Hamilton also worked to ensure his future involvement with skating off the ice. He did the television commentary for the 1985 World Championships in Tokyo, Japan. "I love it but I worry about doing a good job," he later said of commentating.

Despite his contingency plans for the future, a management decision by Ice Capades threw Hamilton into a tailspin in 1986. At the end of that season, Ice Capades decided not to renew his contract. He was still popular, but they let him go because of their belief that people wouldn't consistently buy tickets to see a male skater.

Scott Hamilton was left to ponder his future yet again. In a 1987 interview with Dennis McGovern, he said that he briefly considered giving another branch of show business—acting—a try:

> I went out to L.A. and I was going to find a theatrical agent and take some classes and then I came to a decision over that summer. I saw a lot of actors and a lot of doors slammed in a lot of people's faces and all the stuff you have to go through and I thought I'd rather be a really good skater than a mediocre actor.

That desire to be "a really good skater" was still with Scott Hamilton as he tried to relax on a beach in Florida. He discussed a new career path with his friend Robert Kain, who also happened to be his agent at IMG. Skating with the Ice Capades had been a positive experience for him; but if he had his own touring company, he would do things differently. He would keep striving for continual improvement rather than just settling for a level of skating that he could consistently reach night after night. Surely, Hamilton thought, there were other ice athletes out there who held the same ideal.

Bob Kain thought that the time was right for Scott's concept of a new kind of ice show. Client and agent got to work.

*Scott Hamilton darts across the ice during a professional figure-skating competition. Hamilton created an outlet for professional skaters to showcase their skills with his Scott Hamilton America Tour in 1986; the successful tour's name was eventually changed to Stars on Ice.*

# 7

# STAR ON ICE

"I LOVED CAPADES, had a ball. I wouldn't trade a day I was with them," Hamilton told *American Skating World*. "But I want something now I have a little more control over." His wish had become a reality when the Scott Hamilton America Tour made its way through five New England cities in the fall of 1986. The show featured eight other skaters: Rosalynn Sumners, Sandy Lenz, Brian Pockar, Toller Cranston, Michael Seibert, Judy Blumberg, Lisa Carey, and Chris Harrison. Without a costumed character in sight, the cast performed routines that showcased their technical skills. They also skated in production numbers with entertaining story lines.

The Scott Hamilton America Tour was so successful that the headliner and his agent quickly put together a second tour in December 1986. This time, Olympic gold medalists Dorothy Hamill (1976) and Robin Cousins (1980) joined the company. Hamilton enjoyed playing to smaller crowds than those he had wowed as an amateur. He could establish a rapport with his audiences without giving any thought to pleasing judges.

*Hamilton practices one of his trademark backflips at Wollman Ice Rink in New York City's Central Park. He was in New York practicing for a special Stars on Ice appearance that would benefit terminally ill children through the Make-A-Wish Foundation. Over the years, Hamilton has never forgotten what it felt like to be sick as a child; he has made it a point to donate time and money to organizations such as Make-A-Wish and the American Cancer Society.*

Hamilton's competitive career was by no means over, however. In 1985, Robin Cousins finished just ahead of him to win the NutraSweet World Professional Championships; Hamilton returned the favor in 1986.

Scott Hamilton wanted to keep his competitive sharp edge while enjoying the life of a professional skater. He felt that many big touring ice shows were antithetical to ongoing athletic and artistic growth. The prevalent ice show format did not encourage more than consistent—and sometimes uninspired—performances. There was also a popular perception that professional ice shows were a temporary stop for skaters who were on the road to obscurity.

Hamilton wanted to change that perception. "People used to figure you turn pro, join a show, make money, and fade off into the distance. Things aren't like that anymore. We're all trying to develop and not just rest on our laurels," he said in the February 1987 issue of *American Skating World* magazine. In the same interview, he told writer

Dennis McGovern that his touring company, which was preparing for another run in 1988, served an important purpose in his career. Skating in smaller venues provided Hamilton and his costars an opportunity to try out new routines before professional competitions.

As much as he enjoyed sharing himself with others on the ice, Scott Hamilton came to regret having shared his personal story with journalist Michael Steere. Steere had traveled with him during the emotionally trying 1982 competitive season. At the time, Hamilton was struggling to cope with his celebrity and fighting to defend his newly won national and world titles. Although he had initially cooperated with Steere, sitting for extensive interviews, he eventually withdrew his authorization for the biography.

When *Scott Hamilton: A Behind-the-Scenes Look at the Life and Competitive Times of America's Favorite Figure Skater* was published in late 1985, the book's subject was less than thrilled. "It's just not what I wanted and I don't feel comfortable with it," he commented to *American Skating World*. While he did not feel scandalized by Steere's portrayal of him as relatively moody, he did think that the writer painted an incomplete picture: "I wanted a book more representative of my life and my skating. It didn't even get into the Olympics. It just mainly covered the 1982 season which was difficult and not really representative of the years I've had in skating."

Hamilton added a new chapter to the story of his skating career in the spring of 1987, when he joined the Festival on Ice tour. Festival on Ice featured performances on a small, portable rink placed on a proscenium stage (walled in on three sides, with an open front facing an auditorium). Hamilton was accustomed to skating in arena settings— where he was visible from all sides—but he adapted well to the choreography necessitated by the change of venue. Festival on Ice featured programs with involved story lines, which meant that Hamilton got to try acting on skates.

After wrapping up his stint with Festival on Ice, it was time to prepare a new incarnation of the Scott Hamilton America Tour for another season. This time, Hamilton was not the only one who believed in his power to draw a crowd: Discover Card became his company's corporate sponsor in 1987, and the tour's name was officially changed to Discover Card Stars on Ice. The corporate sponsorship helped ensure the survival of the ice show that Hamilton had cofounded. It also paved the way for some of the highest production values—including standout choreography, and customized costuming and stage lighting—ever seen in professional figure skating. The newly christened Discover Card Stars on Ice played to more markets than it had in 1986, eventually including over 60 cities.

The Stars on Ice Tour forged its most meaningful alliance, however, when it made the Make-A-Wish Foundation its official charity. Make-A-Wish grants the wishes of seriously and terminally ill children. Even today, Hamilton and his costars remain actively involved with the foundation. Stars on Ice regularly donates proceeds to Make-A-Wish; the skaters also take time to brighten the lives of sick children in person.

One grateful family set up a website to thank Scott for the time he spent with their adopted son on two different occasions. "Scott is the essence of what every human being should strive to be. . . . We are especially grateful for what he has done for [our son] and we wish we could help him now," they wrote after learning of his bout with cancer.

From the very inception of Stars on Ice, a large part of Hamilton's appeal was his accessibility and friendliness to fans of all ages. Entertaining the people who came to see him was his main priority. His intuitive belief that other retiring amateur champions would want to join his ice show became fact in 1988. Olympic bronze medalist Debi Thomas was among the new crop of skaters looking for employment in the wake of the Games. She joined Stars on Ice for a time, as did other skaters who were not content to bide their time as their skills declined.

Just two years earlier, Scott Hamilton had been an out-of-work skater soaking up the sun on a Florida beach with his manager; now, Stars on Ice was a figure skating institution with a secure future. As his professional venture grew, Hamilton spent little time looking back on his Olympic glory days. When he was inducted into both the U.S. Olympic Hall of Fame and the World Figure Skating Hall of Fame in 1990, he gave away his 1984 Olympic gold medal. It is now displayed at the World Figure Skating Hall of Fame in Colorado Springs, along with some of his old costumes and skates. "I didn't want the light to shine bright at the Olympics and then get dimmer every year after that," he later explained to *People* magazine.

He may have given away his Olympic medal, but Hamilton showed no signs of being ready to let go of skating. His ice career was still a vital, dynamic work in progress—and still subject to personal ups and downs. After a surprise victory at the Diet Coke Championships on February 17, 1992, in Cincinnati, Ohio, Hamilton spoke with *American Skating World* about his battle against burnout. A series of minor injuries, he explained, had prevented him from training at full capacity and undermined his confidence. He surprised himself and everyone else with a bravura performance in the long program that catapulted him out of fifth place and straight to the top. Hamilton defeated such greats as Viktor Petrenko and Robin Cousins to win.

"For me, the big victory was that I skated as well as I can skate and that I showed to myself that I can still perform under pressure and deliver the goods," he told interviewer Deb Vestal. Although he prevailed this time, Hamilton admitted that an exhausting schedule and confidence problems had been keeping him from the top of his form for some time.

In that same interview, he stated that professional figure skating needed to be systematized—with clear rules on judging, scoring, and payments—as thoroughly as amateur competition was. "We are trying to develop a professional governing body who rule and standardize competitions," he told Vestal.

To that end, Scott Hamilton joined other skating stars in Minneapolis, Minnesota, on June 27, 1992, to formally launch the World Professional Skating Association. The mission statement of the WPSA read: "To enhance professional skating, to provide positive identification with our industry as a sport and art form and to improve and expand the vision of the skating world." Hamilton participated in two days of discussion on such topics as scoring, judging, sponsorship rights, and developing ties to charitable organizations.

Scott Hamilton was in the unique position of being both a current practitioner of his sport and a seasoned, influential figure off of the ice. The magnitude of Hamilton's celebrity showed no signs of fading. Not only was he a featured skater and producer of Stars on Ice; he was also a sought-after commentator. In 1992, CBS hired Scott Hamilton to be its main figure skating commentator at the Olympic Games in Albertville, France. Nobody could better empathize with an Olympic skater's nervousness than Hamilton. "You don't want to be overly critical, because everyone has worked extremely hard," he said before the Olympics. In addition to his obvious compassion for the athletes, he had a brisk, good-humored style in the commentary booth that engaged the interest of TV viewers.

Two years later, Hamilton was again asked to provide Olympic commentary. Before he went to Lillehammer, Norway, for the 1994 Olympic Games, Scott Hamilton reflected on his experiences of a decade earlier. In 1984, Bosnia-Hercegovina had been a republic of Yugoslavia. Sarajevo, the capital of Bosnia-Hercegovina, was under Yugoslavia's Communist rule when it hosted the

Olympics. The city was home to Serbian Orthodox Serbs, Bosnian Muslims, and Roman Catholic Croats. Ten years later, Bosnia-Hercegovina was an independent republic, but it was also being torn apart by bloody ethnic and religious warfare. After Bosnia-Hercegovina gained international recognition as an independent nation in 1992, Bosnian Muslims and Croats joined forces against Serbian attempts to dominate the new country and to create "racial purity" by wiping out all non-Serbs. The once-vital industrial city of Sarajevo was left charred and broken.

The Olympic facilities, where the world had celebrated personal excellence and international cooperation a decade earlier, had become either army quarters or rubble. Zetra Arena was now a United Nations military base. Although saddened by the destruction of the site of his Olympic victory, Hamilton was far more concerned about the fate of Sarajevo's volunteers. In 1984, the Communist Yugoslavian government had required the city's residents to assist in the running of the Olympic Games. Ten years later, many of those volunteers had lost their homes, jobs, and families to brutal warfare. Now, a decade after his Olympic victory, Hamilton and other skaters donated proceeds from their performances to relief efforts in Sarajevo.

As he took his seat in the commentary booth at Lillehammer, the lurid details of the Tonya Harding–Nancy Kerrigan saga were swirling in the air like a blast of winter wind. Kerrigan, one of the top U.S. figure skaters, was attacked after a practice session less than two months before the Olympics. An attacker wielding a lead pipe injured Kerrigan's right knee, nearly keeping her out of the Games. When it was discovered that Harding's former husband had been involved in the attack, many people speculated that the skater had ordered the attack to eliminate her main rival from the Olympic competition. The plan didn't work: Kerrigan was named to the U.S. Olympic figure skating team, along with Harding and an alternate, 13-year-old Michelle Kwan, and her injury was not severe enough to keep her out of the 1994 Games.

The drama transcended the confines of women's figure skating and overshadowed the entire Olympics. Hamilton stuck to the subject—skating—and kept his remarks free of sensationalism as Kerrigan narrowly lost the gold to Oksana Baiul and Harding self-destructed, finishing out of the medals. Harding, her ex-husband, and three other men were later found guilty of criminal conspiracy in the attack.

The Harding-Kerrigan sideshow indirectly benefited

Scott Hamilton: suddenly, people couldn't get enough of televised figure skating. "I'm sitting around in the summer of 1995 . . . and my telephone starts ringing off the hook," he told the *Honolulu Star-Bulletin*. "When you're 11 years out [of the Olympics] and that happens, you know something is changing big time."

But before Hamilton could reap the rewards of increasing interest in professional skating performances and competitions, he had to weather a devastating loss that he learned of while still in Lillehammer. On the last day of Olympic competition, he learned that his father had died. Ernie Hamilton, who was residing in Florida, had been in chronically poor health for some time. His death was nonetheless a shock to his oldest adopted son, who immediately left Norway for Florida. Ernie's funeral was held in Bowling Green, where he had been a respected professor, a devoted father, and an avid volunteer for the Bowling Green Skating Club's Ice Horizons shows.

Show business waited for no one, however. Hamilton had a Stars on Ice show to do in New York City's Madison Square Garden on the evening after the funeral. He somehow managed to charm the crowd that night after a day of personal sorrow.

The spring of 1994 brought Hamilton back to Bowling Green under happier circumstances. He had been invited to speak to the graduating class of Bowling Green State University. Dr. Sam Cooper, a faculty member and long-time friend, awarded Scott an honorary doctorate of performing arts.

Scott Hamilton had come far since his teenage years, when he had scrambled to piece together the required courses to graduate from high school. Skating demanded a great deal from him, but it also gave him a great deal in return. His life off the ice had become another source of satisfaction. Hamilton had been involved with girlfriend Karen Plage since the late 1980s. Plage's father was Hamilton's friend, and Karen, who was a teenager when

*Hamilton receives an hon-orary degree from Bowling Green University in 1994. The skater spoke to that year's graduating class at the col-lege where both his father and mother had taught.*

she first met Scott in 1981, later told *People*, "I always liked to be around when Scott was around, but I didn't know why. Now I've got the man I want."

Hamilton also cherished the friendships he forged with his Stars on Ice costars. Some of these relationships were now in their second decade: Rosalynn Sumners, for exam-ple, had skated in the first Scott Hamilton America Tour and was still a member of Stars on Ice. The company had become a second family to him.

Like any other family, however, the Stars on Ice com-pany was vulnerable to tragedy. On November 20, 1995, married pairs skaters Ekaterina Gordeeva, 24, and Sergei Grinkov, 28, were practicing in Lake Placid, New York, in preparation for a new season. As they were practicing a routine lift, Gordeeva was surprised when Grinkov's arms failed to encircle her waist. Her partner collapsed on the ice; minutes later, the powerful young skater was dead from a massive heart attack.

In her autobiography, *My Sergei: A Love Story*, Ekaterina Gordeeva recalled Hamilton's comforting presence during her darkest days of young widowhood. He accompanied her to Grinkov's viewing. "I brought Scott in myself," she wrote. "He had always tried very hard to get Sergei to laugh, and Sergei felt comfortable with him."

Although he was not yet middle-aged, people looked to Scott Hamilton as a mature voice of reason in the youth-oriented world of figure skating. When sports reporter Christine Brennan's controversial look at figure skating, *Inside Edge*, hit bookstores in 1996, the USFSA temporarily barred her from covering all sanctioned skating events. *Inside Edge* examined the 1994–95 figure skating season and how the Harding-Kerrigan brouhaha helped put televised skating on the map. Brennan also trained a critical eye on judging practices in amateur competition, and asserted that AIDS was quietly killing off male performers and choreographers, devastating the sport.

Hamilton disagreed with Brennan's claims that homosexuality and AIDS were more prevalent among skaters than among other segments of the population. Still, he criticized the USFSA's decision to banish Christine Brennan from its events. "Isn't freedom of the press guaranteed?" he asked rhetorically.

Although people valued his opinions, even an influential athlete and entertainer like Scott Hamilton sometimes had trouble convincing people of the feasibility of his ideas. Despite the fact that he had done six skating specials for Disney, he spent almost 13 years vainly pitching the idea of a TV variety show on ice. He told the Associated Press that he first met with a negative response to the idea in 1984: "They said variety was dead, that a male figure skater never would have a prime-time special, to let it go, that it was a bad idea," he remembered. "So it was just one of those things I fantasized about."

*The skater strikes an entertaining pose during his 1997 television special "Disney's Scott Hamilton . . . Upside Down." The program received good ratings, raves from fans, and an Emmy Award for choreography.*

Hamilton's years of wishful thinking became reality on March 8, 1997 when "Disney's Scott Hamilton . . . Upside Down" aired on CBS Television. "I waited 13 years for this, and I think it's one of the most unique TV specials done for American television," he said. Teaming up with his Stars on Ice colleagues, Hamilton played a chimney sweep from *Mary Poppins*, a Zamboni driver, and Charlie Chaplin, to name just a few of his roles in the hour-long program.

"Scott Hamilton . . . Upside Down" received good ratings and raves for dazzling special effects like those in Hamilton's salute to Fred Astaire, in which he appeared to be skating up the walls of an elevator. Choreographer Sarah Kawahara, with whom he had been working steadi-

ly for more than a decade, won an Emmy award for her
work on "Scott Hamilton . . . Upside Down."

The man who before the 1984 Olympics had mused,
"Look at all the neat things that have happened to me,"
probably couldn't have forseen the prosperity and success
that would be his in 1997. Scott Hamilton had continued
to make "neat" things happen in his life. But as winter
gave way to spring, his jumps weren't coming quite as eas-
ily as they always had. He tried to ignore the pain in his
abdomen and back as he toured with Stars on Ice. Perhaps
it was an ulcer, he rationalized—not an unlikely possibili-
ty, given his hectic schedule.

As an elite athlete, Hamilton was accustomed to working through pain. But when it got so agonizing that standing upright became difficult after a March 15 show in East
Lansing, Michigan, he knew that the time for rationaliza-
tion had ended.

*Despite a diagnosis of testicular cancer in March 1997, Scott Hamilton always felt that he could return to figure skating. "I don't want this episode to stop me from skating," he said in an interview. "When I no longer enjoy it, I will stop. . . . I love my job and that is inspiration enough."*

# 8

# OVERCOMING ONCE MORE

"AFTER THE SHOW that night I was in such pain that I couldn't stand up straight," Hamilton later told *People*. The next stop for Stars on Ice was Peoria, Illinois. On March 16, he went to that city's St. Francis Medical Center for tests. There, he learned that the source of his pain and difficulty on the ice was a tumor twice the size of a grape-fruit. The words of the doctor who treated him reverberated in his ears: "If it were me, I would take care of this immediately."

But Hamilton had a show to do. He kept his secret throughout the March 16 performance, skating with the dreadful knowledge that this just might be his last hurrah on the ice. "I actually skated great," he remembered. On another occasion, he told the *Denver Post*, "Getting through that show probably taught me a lot about myself, and helped me a great deal in facing the next four and a half months."

After the show, Hamilton broke the news to the other skaters. That night, he departed for the Cleveland Clinic Foundation, a cancer treat-ment center where he would undergo tests the next day. The hardest task that Hamilton faced was telling his longtime girlfriend, Karen

*The support of friends and fellow Stars on Ice performers such as (from left) Kurt Browning, Kristi Yamaguchi, and Katerina Witt helped Scott Hamilton through the difficult period of recovery from cancer.*

Plage. Plage was at their home in suburban Denver when she received a phone call from Hamilton. "She cried—and then she realized the worst thing she could do was be scared and weak," he said.

Hamilton and Plage were together at the Cleveland Clinic the next day when they heard the diagnosis: testicular cancer. "I was scared and a little blown away by the news," he recalled. In an attempt at deadpan humor, Hamilton asked his somber-looking doctors, "Is that all it is?"

In fact, his condition was potentially life-threatening. Testicular cancer accounts for only about one percent of all cancers in American men, striking some 7,000 in the United States annually. Although when treated early testicular cancer can be cured 80 to 90 percent of the time, the disease typically strikes men in their twenties to forties—men prone to delay treatment because they take good health for granted. Hamilton's case was a textbook example of how a relatively curable disease could turn deadly. He had been feeling unwell for weeks before seeking treatment, procrastinating until he became unable to pursue his normal activities. The price he paid for waiting was a large, malignant tumor. The doctors at the Cleveland Clinic urged Hamilton to start treatment at once.

The Olympic gold medalist whose mother never lived to see his glory couldn't help but think of her now. He remembered the pain Dorothy Hamilton had endured as breast cancer invaded her entire body. All of her bravery did not spare her from incredible suffering; now, her son feared the same fate.

The tumor in his abdomen was inoperable because of its size, so the goal of Hamilton's oncologist, Dr. Ronald Bukowski, was to shrink it. Chemotherapy was the main weapon used against Hamilton's cancer. Dr. Bukowski would administer the chemical treatment in four 5-day cycles, with 16-day breaks between treatments. That added up to about four months of enduring, waiting, and hoping for the best.

Before he began his first round of chemotherapy on March 21, the story of Scott Hamilton's cancer diagnosis had already made headlines. He later described the surreal experience of coming across TV coverage of his condition. "I was back in the hotel after it was announced," he told *USA Today*. "I was channel-surfing and it was the lead story. I was blown away. It was scary, like they knew something I didn't. I thought I better write myself a card."

His legions of friends and fans in the skating world were shocked. "Scott is the symbol of eternal youth in skating," observed ABC skating commentator Dick Button. "It comes as a real blow to realize that your symbol is under attack."

*While undergoing cancer therapy, Hamilton received thousands of cards from friends and well-wishers. The outpouring of support is understandable, given all that Hamilton had done for others during his career. He is pictured here at a 1995 benefit for children with AIDS.*

Although chemotherapy was not pleasant, Hamilton said that to his surprise, he "didn't find it to be horrible." On treatment days, he received injections from 10:00 A.M. to 4:00 P.M. The chemicals were toxic; there was no way to kill the tumor without exposing healthy tissue to the drugs, too. After the injections, he was free to leave the hospital until 11:00 P.M., when he was readmitted for the night. He slept connected to an IV drip to prevent dehydration.

Hamilton later said that laughing a lot was key to his recovery. Even the hospital personnel did what they could to lighten what was a potentially grave situation. During a November 4, 1997, appearance on *The Late Late Show with Tom Snyder*, he said that the nurses who administered his chemotherapy drew cartoon characters on his IV bags.

Eating well was also important. Although anti-nausea medications he took between treatments dulled his appetite, Hamilton found that during chemotherapy cycles he frequently craved "chicken, burgers and Chinese."

Some of the other difficulties associated with chemotherapy caught up with Hamilton after the first treatment. Although he felt bloated after each round of treatment, his actual body weight was decreasing. The drugs also sapped his energy and caused his hair to start falling out.

Before he began his second cycle of chemotherapy, he enlisted Karen's help in heading off one of the treatment's side effects: she shaved his head before the drugs took all of his hair, clump by clump. "For a while, if you squinted real hard, I looked like Michael Jordan," he later cracked. Hamilton credits Plage with pulling him through the months of chemotherapy by keeping abreast of his treatment protocol, managing his medical paperwork, and encouraging him to eat whether he felt like it or not. "Karen, who is studying acting and singing in Denver, was there for me 24 hours a day," Hamilton told *People*. "I always tell everybody she's much better than I deserve."

He needed Karen's support more and more as chemotherapy progressed. As his doctors predicted, Hamilton found the third round to be the toughest. With his fourth and final treatment remaining, he told himself, "everyone can do something for one last time."

In addition to Karen Plage, Scott Hamilton relied on a few close friends. His costars from Stars on Ice had visited him the day after his cancer was diagnosed, using their day off to buoy his spirits with jokes and companionship. And he received thousands of cards from fans, acquaintences, and admirers. When Hamilton was hospitalized, his publicist brought him some of the avalanche of cards and

*Although the treatment to eliminate his testicular cancer was successful, Scott Hamilton knew that his recovery would not be complete until he could perform on the ice again.*

letters sent by well-wishers. "I've heard from everybody I've ever met in my life," he later marveled. "It's really made me realize how lucky I am."

While he was going through his illness, though, Hamilton felt that the cancer was even harder on his loved ones than on him. He allowed his younger brother Steve to visit him in Cleveland but kept other relatives away. "They were upset and felt I was acting selfish," he said of their reaction. "But I wanted to keep this period in my life as private as possible."

Hamilton described himself as "scared out of my mind" on June 22. That was the day he flew back to Cleveland for surgery. The chemotherapy had done its job: the germ cell tumor in his abdomen had shrunk to the size of a golf ball.

On June 24, Dr. Eric Klein made an incision from just below Hamilton's sternum (breastbone) to just above his groin in order to remove the tumor; Klein also removed the lymph nodes around the tumor to prevent the spread of any remaining cancerous cells. The surgeon made another incision in Hamilton's groin area to take out the right testicle.

Although his surgery was successful, Scott Hamilton's uphill battle was far from over. "The day after surgery the pain kicked in—like Pow! I couldn't sit up," he told *People*. During the eight-day hospital stay that followed the operation, he waited for his intestines to begin functioning normally again. The surgeon had moved them from their normal position to reach the tumor, and Hamilton was unable to eat solid food for the remainder of his hospitalization.

The four-time world champion later said he never doubted that he would beat cancer; overcoming the residual effects of his treatment was another matter. Although he had already resumed skating when he shared his story in the September 8 issue of *People* magazine, he still was a long way from recapturing his former strength and energy. "My doctors say I have to be patient and it could take a long time to come back," Hamilton said. But in the same article, he also said, "I've got to keep pushing it," betraying the dogged persistence and unwillingness to accept anything less than excellence that had propelled him to the top of the figure skating world in the first place. In another interview not long after his surgery, Scott Hamilton stated his mission in no uncertain terms: "I don't want this episode to stop me from skating. When I no longer enjoy it, I will stop. . . . I love my job and that is inspiration enough."

Only his love for his job could adequately explain the struggles that Hamilton voluntarily endured to get back on the ice.

*Scott Hamilton in an upbeat mood after his successful comeback from cancer.*

# 9

# "SCURRY MODE"

SCOTT HAMILTON MAY have survived his bout with testicular cancer, but he still considered the victory incomplete. "I don't like to lose," he told several interviewers during his convalescence. Anything less than a full return to the ice would fall short of winning.

During chemotherapy, Hamilton had been forbidden to skate because his doctors feared that the medications he was taking would compromise his balance. Surgery had further delayed his return, forcing him to wait until his abdominal incision had healed. He was finally allowed to skate again on August 1, 1997. It wasn't until August 9, however, that he summoned the nerve to lace up a new pair of skates at a rink in Simi Valley, California.

Over the course of Hamilton's nearly 30-year skating career, his body had become the eager servant to whatever moves his mind could visualize. He quickly realized that everything had changed. "My body just didn't want to work," he remembered. Both his strength and balance were gone. Even the most basic spins and jumps were out of the question at first. With him on the Simi Valley ice was his longtime

*Hamilton caught a bouquet of flowers from Canadian ice dancer Shae-Lynn Bourne while he was sitting rinkside at an exhibition performance during the 1998 Winter Olympics in Nagano, Japan. He is loved by other skaters as much as by fans because of all that he has done for his sport as a skater, commentator, and tour promoter.*

choreographer, Sarah Kawahara. He later recalled feeling self-conscious about his inability to skate well, even though his doctors had warned him that regaining his former level of performance would take a very long time.

His skills gradually came back to him. In less than a week, Hamilton could do some double jumps. "It ain't much, but everything I've got is pure skating muscle," he had quipped to *Sports Illustrated* in 1984; now, he needed to regain that muscle. He planned a weight training regimen to build up his frame, which cancer treatments had diminished to 115 pounds. He had about two months to prepare himself for his October comeback performance, a benefit for the Cleveland Clinic Foundation.

As he prepared for his first postcancer performance, Hamilton broke his silence about the ordeal he had just faced. "I didn't want to talk to anybody when I was in the middle of it," he told the *Las Vegas Sun*, "but when I was past it, I felt I had something to say. I felt that maybe I could offer some enlightenment to how it all works, what it does to you physically, and offer understanding to people who have friends going through cancer."

Now that his was a voice of optimism, Hamilton began to talk. He kept interviewers posted on his progress as he prepared for his comeback. He was candid in his assessments: "Right now, I would be competitive with a six-year-old," he told the *Detroit Free Press*'s Jo-Ann Barnas in September. Although he was learning to consider his illness "a very short and very temporary" episode in his life, Hamilton did not discount its seriousness. The climb back to top form wasn't always steady. He later told *USA Today* that at one point, he "was skating like a cancer survivor instead of a healthy person." He had to find enough courage to break through the tentativeness that still held him back. After the scar tissue on his stomach healed, Scott Hamilton toiled to reclaim the backflip as his personal trademark.

Hamilton used the attention paid to his comeback to encourage men to take responsibility for their health. He urged other men to avoid the mistake he made in delaying treatment. He told the *Las Vegas Sun*:

> I knew I was having trouble. I *thought* it was an ulcer. I *thought* I could put it off until later. I *thought* the problems were lifestyle-related. I *never* thought I would have cancer. It was like, duh, I guess this kind of thing *can* happen to me.

When "Scott Hamilton: Back on the Ice" aired on CBS on November 5, 1997, it was the 20th most popular program on television that week. The broadcast of his October 29 comeback performance attracted nearly 17 million viewers.

Skating fans eagerly awaited Hamilton's return to Stars on Ice. His determination to regain his former level of performance on the tour grew stronger as he watched his friends develop routines for the coming season. Stars on Ice offered Hamilton the opportunity to do part-time guest appearances until he felt ready to take on more. However, unwilling to settle for less than a total commitment to the company he had helped found, Hamilton turned down the offer, electing instead to keep training until he could rejoin Stars on Ice full time.

By Thanksgiving, Hamilton returned to the Stars on Ice tour. When the show stopped in Spokane, Washington, on January 4, 1998, the *Spokesman-Review* gave it high marks. Writer Susan English singled Hamilton out for particular praise. "None of the skaters . . . was more loved by his audience than Scott Hamilton," she observed. When he skated his comeback number, "With One More Look at You," the crowd was profoundly affected, English noted. "The audience fell silent, and some tears slid down cheeks," English wrote. "He is, indeed, the quintessential entertainer and an inspiring man."

As the winter of 1998 unfolded, Hamilton was in his self-described "scurry mode." His determination to make a complete recovery had transformed itself into restlessness. "I think if I do it quicker, faster, harder, everything will be better. But it's not. Right now, nothing seems second nature yet," he had told *USA Today* in the late fall of 1997.

Whenever Hamilton weighed in with an opinion on figure skating, people listened. He had pushed to uphold professional figure skating's legitimacy as a sport—by calling for a uniform governing body and ironclad rules—ever since leaving the amateur ranks. Although long gone from amateur competition, the 1984 gold medalist was an avid observer of contemporary developments.

In her 1998 book, *Edge of Glory*, Christine Brennan quotes Hamilton's misgivings about the 1990 elimination of the compulsory figures segment from amateur competition. As a youngster, practicing figures had hardly been a favorite activity; as a veteran, he appreciated how the painstaking repetition of figures had matured him as a

skater. "When you have something that takes that long to perfect," Hamilton said, "you have champions who wait their turn and really learn their craft. Now, if you've got a triple jump, you can win tomorrow."

He was also concerned about the tendency among the new crop of skaters to prize jumps above overall program content. As men struggled to execute clean quadruple jumps in competition, for example, Hamilton felt that their presentation and "in-between" skating suffered. The trend towards singleminded obsession with jumping was a departure from Hamilton's long-held belief that a program should be uniquely personal and artistic first, packed with dazzling jumps second.

In February 1998, Scott Hamilton got a chance to talk about up-and-coming ice stars from around the world when he returned to the CBS commentator's chair for the 1998

*Hamilton covers his face in surprise at the announcement that he had been selected to the Madison Square Garden Walk of Fame in March 1998. With him are friends and fellow skaters Jayne Torvill, Kurt Browning, Ekaterina Gordeeva, Rosalynn Sumners, and Elena Bechke.*

*Scott Hamilton: Still leaping, spinning, and holding the hearts of figure skating fans everywhere.*

Winter Olympic Games in Nagano, Japan. By now, it was difficult for television viewers to imagine watching the Olympic figure skating events without Hamilton's sharp, affable presence in the booth offering honest, yet compassionate appraisals of each skater's performance—good or bad.

As he covered the events in Nagano, Hamilton admitted that he still felt more tired than usual. He said that he was trying to safeguard his energy, although he maintained a schedule that would make almost anyone else's head spin. He was also busy perfecting a routine that he'd developed in the fall, in which he portrayed every character in *The Wizard of Oz*. The long amateur programs that once challenged Hamilton's endurance as a young man ran four-and-a-half minutes; this one ran a staggering six-and-a-half minutes.

As he took on more and more, the venerated champion occasionally doubted his own common sense. "I've fried my lungs with chemotherapy. I've got no legs. . . . Why am I doing this?" he wondered aloud of his decision to skate the *Wizard of Oz* program on tour.

Hamilton turned his sense of humor on himself, gently ridiculing his tendency to pile one accomplishment on top of another in an endless flurry of activity. "I got past a childhood illness. I won an Olympic gold medal. And I've gotten past cancer. With those three things, what's next? An Academy Award?!" he cracked in September 1997 on NBC's *Dateline*.

Given his many recent endeavors, a future Oscar doesn't seem so far-fetched. One of the numerous projects in Scott Hamilton's plans for 1999 was a proposed skating show on

Broadway. He was also preparing an autobiography for publication. He had already tried his hand at writing, contributing the foreword to Kristi Yamaguchi's *Figure Skating for Dummies*.

Commentator, producer, writer: Scott Hamilton was wearing all of these hats in 1998. First and foremost, however, he was still an entertainer. On the night of March 28, Hamilton participated in The Great Skate Debate at the University of Illinois ice arena. This was a professional competition with a twist: the audience did the judging. It was an event he had won before. As he pantomimed, acted, spun, and jumped through the entire dramatis personae of *The Wizard of Oz*, his ebullience and comedic talent left the audience little choice but to root for Scott Hamilton.

Still winded from his grueling program, the champion said that the Great Skate Debate was a celebration rather than a competition. He gratefully acknowledged the affection showered on him by the crowd, saying that it made him "want to skate forever."

To be sure, there are many who fervently wish right along with Scott Hamilton that he could skate forever. In a sport that produces ever-younger champions, he has come close to doing so. His valiant battle with cancer was just one moment in a lifetime of overcoming obstacles. This—along with his personal grace and good humor—is the secret of Scott Hamilton's appeal: he is the scrawny weakling who transformed himself into the king of the ice by virtue of hard work. He has graciously accepted the world's adulation without forgetting how to cope with whatever difficulties may befall him.

"Life is an adventure," he told *USA Today* as he emerged from his fearsome brush with mortality. "Every day there's a brand new challenge. Whatever it is, it's never a cakewalk. It's not meant to be easy, and I learned it's not supposed to be fair."

Whether or not the rest of his career is easy or fair, Scott Hamilton is sure to make a worthwhile adventure of it.

# APPENDIX

## CANCER-RELATED ORGANIZATIONS

**The Scott Hamilton Fund**
Cleveland Clinic Cancer Center-T40
9500 Euclid Avenue
Cleveland, Ohio 44195

The following is a list of organizations in the United States that are involved in cancer research and/or provide support and assistance to victims of cancer and their families.

**American Cancer Society**
1599 Clifton Road, NE
Atlanta, GA 30329
(800) ACS-2345
www.cancer.org

**American Institute for Cancer Research**
1759 R St. NW
Washington, DC 20009
(800) 843-8114
aicrweb@aicr.org
www.aicr.org

**Cancer Care, Inc.**
1180 Avenue of the Americas
2nd Floor
New York, NY 10036
(800) 813-HOPE
www.cancercareinc.org

**Cancer Research Foundation of America**
1600 Duke St.
Alexandria, VA 22314
(703) 836-4412
www.preventcancer.org

**Cancer Support Community**
350 Bay St., Box 100-358
San Francisco, CA 94133
mlight@sj.bigger.net
www.cancersupportcommunity.org

**Candlelighters Childhood Cancer Foundation**
2025 I St. NW
Washington, DC 20006
(202) 659-5136

**International Association of Cancer Counselors**
Jannus Associates
1800 Augusta St., Suite 150
Houston, TX 77057
(713) 780-1057

**National Cancer Institute**
National Institutes of Health
9000 Rockville Pike, Building 31, 10A24
Bethesda, MD 20892
(301) 496-5583
Cancer Information Hotline:
(800) 4-CANCER (9:00 AM-4:30 PM EST)
(800) 638-6694 (24 hours a day)
www.nci.nih.gov

**Y-ME National Breast Cancer Organization, Inc.**
212 Van Buren St.
Chicago, IL 60607-3908
Office Phone: (312) 986-8338
Office Fax: (312) 294-8597
National Hotline: (800) 221-2141
Spanish Hotline: (800) 986-9505
help@y-me.org
www.y-me.org

# FURTHER READING

Barnas, Jo-Ann. "Tripped by Cancer, Hamilton Lands on Skates." *Detroit Free Press*, 16 September 1997.

Becker, Debbie. "Hamilton Fights Cancer with Confidence." *USA Today*, 16 September 1997.

———. "Skater's Life Returning to Normal after Battle with Cancer." *USA Today*, 28 November 1997.

Borsuk, Alan J. "Nothing Can Keep Hamilton from Dazzling a Crowd." *Milwaukee Journal Sentinel*, 26 February 1998.

Brennan, Christine. *Edge of Glory: The Inside Story of the Quest for Skating's Olympic Gold Medals*. New York: Scribner, 1998.

———. *Inside Edge: A Revealing Journey into the Secret World of Figure Skating*. New York: Scribner, 1996.

English, Susan. "Hamilton, Colleagues Glisten in Stars on Ice." *The Spokesman-Review*, 6 January 1998.

Frei, Terry. "Hamilton Fights to Return to the Ice." The *Denver Post*, 16 September 1997.

Gordeeva, Ekaterina, and E. M. Swift. *My Sergei: A Love Story*. New York: Warner Books, 1996.

"Great Scott Won't Be Sold Short." *Newsweek*, 13 February 1984.

"Hamilton Hoping to Return to Tour Soon." Associated Press, 16 September 1997.

Hamilton, Scott. Interview by Stone Phillips. *Dateline*. NBC Television, 2 September 1997.

———. Interview by Tom Snyder. *The Late Late Show with Tom Snyder*. NBC Television, 4 November 1997.

Hamilton, Scott, and Lorenzo Benet. "Fighting Heart." *People*, 8 September 1997.

"Hamilton Hoping to Return to Tour Soon." Associated Press, 16 September 1997.

"Hamilton's TV Special Fulfills a Dream." Associated Press, 3 March 1997.

Harris, Beth. "Hamilton Prepares for First Post-Cancer Show." Associated Press, 27 October 1997.

Holtz, Randy. "Hamilton's Latest Victory the Most Important." Scripps Howard News Service, 16 September 1997.

McGovern, Dennis. "Scott Hamilton Has Something to Offer." *American Skating World*, February 1987.

Oppegaard, Brett. "Go Figure." *The Columbian*, 1 January 1998.

Ottum, Bob. "Great Scott!" *Sports Illustrated*, 21 March 1983.

———. "Wow! Power." *Sports Illustrated*, 6 February 1984.

Ryan, Tim. "Skating Cool Work, If You Can Get it." *Honolulu Star-Bulletin*, 6 June 1996.

Schorr, Melissa. "Fire and Ice with Scott Hamilton." *Las Vegas Sun*, 21 October 1997.

Shaughnessy, Linda. *Scott Hamilton: Fireworks on Ice*. Parsippany, N.J.: Crestwood House, 1998.

Steere, Michael. *Scott Hamilton: A Behind-the-Scenes Look at the Life and Competitive Times of America's Favorite Figure Skater*. New York: St. Martin's Press, 1985.

Summerall, Pat, Jim Moskovitz, and Craig Kubey. *Sports in America*. New York: Harper-Collins, 1996.

"Up Front: Snow Business." *People*, 17 February 1992.

Vestal, Deb. "A Talk with Scott." *American Skating World*, August 1992.

Wilner, Barry. "Hamilton Knew He'd Beat Cancer." *Bergen Record*, 17 September 1997.

Wilner, Barry and Scott Hamilton. *Stars on Ice: The Story of the Champions Tour*. Kansas City: Andrews McMeel, 1998.

# CHRONOLOGY

| | |
|---|---|
| 1958 | Scott Scovell Hamilton born on August 28; adopted in October by Dr. Ernest ("Ernie") and Dorothy Hamilton |
| 1967 | Suffering from a chronic gastrointestinal illness with no known cause, Scott tries ice skating at Bowling Green's newly constructed rink |
| 1968 | His health restored, Scott begins skating lessons at Bowling Green; skates in first performance |
| 1969 | First coach, Rita Lowery, departs Bowling Green; replaced by Giuliano Grassi |
| 1970 | Herb Plata becomes Scott's coach; Scott wins Regional Championships at Juvenile level; competes in Golden West Championships in Culver City, California, as both singles skater and ice dancer |
| 1972 | Wins second regional title; leaves Plata and Bowling Green to train at Wagon Wheel Resort in Rockton, Illinois, under Pierre Brunet; qualifies for National Championships at Novice level |
| 1973 | Qualifies for second National Championships as Novice skater; finishes ninth out of ten |
| 1974 | Rehabilitates injured right ankle; Dorothy Hamilton diagnosed with breast cancer |
| 1975 | Advances to Junior level; qualifies for National Championships, finishes seventh; Pierre Brunet retires; Scott briefly coached by Mary Ludington and Evy Scotvold |
| 1976 | Hamilton family unable to afford Scott's continued skating; Scott wins Junior National Championships; prominent coach Carlo Fassi connects Scott with benefactors willing to fund his skating career, then takes on Scott as pupil at Denver's Colorado Ice Arena; Scott graduates high school; passes last figure test and advances to Senior level |
| 1977 | Battling injury, qualifies for Nationals but places ninth at competition; Dorothy Hamilton dies May 19 |
| 1978 | Wins bronze medal at National Championships, which qualifies him for Worlds in Ottawa; finishes in 11th place |
| 1979 | Reinjures right ankle; fails to qualify for World Championships; relocates to Philadelphia and switches to coach Don Laws; wins Flaming Leaves competition in Lake Placid, New York |
| 1980 | Wins bronze medal at National Championships and qualifies for 1980 Winter Olympic Games at Lake Placid, where he carries the American flag in opening ceremonies; places fifth overall; places fifth at World Championships; skates in |

first Bowling Green ice show to benefit American Cancer Society; follows coach Don Laws to Denver's Colorado Ice Arena

1981    Wins 1981 Nationals; Ernie Hamilton suffers stroke during the competition; wins 1981 Worlds

1982    Wins 1982 Nationals and Worlds

1983    Wins 1983 Nationals and Worlds; begins wearing simple costume in response to increasingly flashy attire in men's figure skating

1984    Wins 1984 Nationals and qualifies for the 1984 Winter Olympics in Sarajevo, Yugoslavia, where he wins gold medal on February 16; wins 1984 Worlds; announces retirement from amateur competition in March; coaches briefly before signing with Ice Capades

1985    Michael Steere's unauthorized biography of Hamilton published

1986    Ice Capades elects not to continue Hamilton's contract; Hamilton and agent Robert Kain launch Scott Hamilton America Tour

1987    Joins Festival on Ice Tour; Discover Card becomes corporate sponsor of Hamilton's new touring company, Stars on Ice

1990    Inducted into both the U.S. Olympic and World Figure Skating Halls of Fame

1992    Provides CBS's commentary for 1992 Winter Olympics in Albertville, Canada; joins other skaters at conference in Minneapolis to form World Professional Skating Association

1994    Serves as CBS commentator for 1994 Olympics in Lillehammer, Norway; Receives honorary doctorate in performing arts from Bowling Green State University

1997    "Scott Hamilton . . . Upside Down" airs on CBS March 8; diagnosed with testicular cancer in March and undergoes chemotherapy; has surgery on June 24; resumes skating in August; skates comeback performance in California on October 29; rejoins Stars on Ice in November

1998    Does CBS commentary for 1998 Winter Olympics in Nagano, Japan; wins the Great Skate Debate on March 28; writes book *Stars on Ice: The Story of the Champions' Tour*, published in November

# INDEX

# PICTURE CREDITS

**KRISTINE BRENNAN** is a writer and editor who lives in the Philadelphia area with her husband and son. She holds a B.A. in English with a concentration in professional writing from Elizabethtown College. She is also the author of *Diana, Princess of Wales* in Chelsea House's WOMEN OF ACHIEVEMENT series.

**JAMES SCOTT BRADY** serves on the board of trustees with the Center to Prevent Handgun Violence and is the Vice Chairman of the Brain Injury Foundation. Mr. Brady served as Assistant to the President and White House Press Secretary under President Ronald Reagan. He was severely injured in an assassination attempt on the president, but remained the White House Press Secretary until the end of the administration. Since leaving the White House, Mr. Brady has lobbied for stronger gun laws. In November 1993, President Bill Clinton signed the Brady Bill, a national law requiring a waiting period on handgun purchases and a background check on buyers.